The Five Drivers of

Digital Marketing

for

Brick and Mortar Businesses

by

Anthony Sakovich

FIVE DRIVERS OF BUSINESS MARKETING ONLINE

Introduction

I would be incredibly satisfied if all small business owners were able to run their own comprehensive online marketing programs.

Too many people see online marketing as a mystical science, bordering on magic. Google hasn't done much to dispel this myth, with its talk of algorithms, Panda, BERT, Knowledge Panel, and Passage Indexing. Many small business owners only know that there is a random element to it, and because the jargon is so unfamiliar, they often turn over the work to other people, and simply hope it will eventually work.

But that's not doing things in the right order. It's not until you understand the moving parts of online business marketing that you can intelligently hire someone else to do it. There is a basic foundation that you can build for yourself, and once you get beyond those basics, you can make an informed decision on precisely what help you need, and what performance requirements you can expect of them. You can do this because, contrary to popular opinion, business marketing online is nothing like any marketing you've ever done before. In fact, I'm here to say that Business Marketing Online is like no other marketing you've ever encountered.

In fact, it's easier.

Unfortunately, we tend to think of it like traditional advertising platforms. It is nothing of the sort, and that is the cause of a lot of the confusion. It is, in fact, such a purified version of theoretical marketing that it is virtually unrecognizable to anyone who has been doing traditional marketing and advertising for their small businesses. In the classic model, you might have done well doing print advertising in the local newspaper. Then, you'd add radio, and see if it increased your business. If that didn't work, then maybe you'd switch to a few months of direct mail campaigns, or the yellow pages, or broadcast tv, or cable. You would wonder what worked, and frequently base your decisions upon the last customer you talked to and whether she had seen your ad on television or not. You simply couldn't know where people were coming from, so you just spent money on anything that seemed to generate any kind of response.

Online marketing is entirely different. Online marketing is like having your own research and testing facility for marketing right at your fingertips. There isn't ANY part of online marketing that won't work for your business, and you have the luxury to test them for very little, even no money. Since you can now check the performance of every piece of marketing against any benchmark you wish to set, you can know exactly what doesn't work so you can stop it, and what things you need to be doing a lot more of because they are producing results.

You can start an online business marketing program with absolutely no money out of pocket. The more money you have, the faster you can grow your business, that's all. But the beauty of it is that you don't really need any money to start. The marketing laboratory comparison I made above is not actually an analogy. It's an accurate description of what you have at your fingertips. For the inventors and entrepreneurs in the audience, that will give them an immense sense of hope and comfort, as they are frequently at home with the idea of testing, iterations and modifications.

For a regular retailer, it can be a little intimidating, but really, it's the biggest liberator you'll ever encounter. Why's that? Because, quite simply, it means you can never, ever make a mistake. Nothing EVER costs you money any more. It just affects how much money you make.

There are two ways to look at the world. The work of Dr. Carol Dweck at Columbia University on learning perspectives can most easily be summed up by a comparison of the following two phrases. One represents a fixed mindset, the other a growth mindset. When you read them, you'll figure out which is which with little difficulty.

"Sometimes you win, sometimes you lose."

versus

"Sometimes you win, *sometimes you learn*."

With online business marketing, you only lose when you stop marketing. How can that be? Simply put, even if your marketing campaign generates zero response, then you have, at the very least, learned a way to NOT do your marketing. It doesn't matter. It just didn't work...that way.

The beauty of the Five Drivers system is that you are doing this work yourself, for the most part, so there is no real cost to the program except your time. As you start to develop new programs and start to get some level of success, you will now have your own set of benchmarks you can use to see if your latest changes work better or worse than what you've been doing to that point. If it doesn't work as well, then chuck the new program and create another new one. If it is an improvement over your previous methods, you chuck the old one in favor of the new one. It's that simple. There's no "but it's my baby!" feeling, because they are all just samples in ongoing marketing tests.

So, if you have a desire to grow your business, and you have a willingness to experiment with your ideas for how to best market it, then online business marketing is the best thing to happen to your business in the last hundred years or more. In fact, it is the first major revolution in marketing we've had since it became a serious field of study.

That probably explains why people are so perplexed by it. Everything appears to be magic until you figure out the science that makes it work.

About the Five Drivers

My name is Anthony Sakovich, and I didn't invent the Five Drivers of Business Marketing Online... but I did discover them. I wasn't the first to discover them, either. My goal, however, is to be the best at *explaining* them, so that you can use these five basic internet marketing functions to grow your own "brick and mortar" business using the power of the web. Why should you listen to me, as opposed to the thousands of web gurus, advice blogs and technology forums? I think that question answers itself, really. There isn't one place for you to turn where you can get a "whole course" in online business marketing. You would have to do as I did: spend three years, and over a hundred thousand dollars, analyzing all the data and coming up with your own solution. I hope this book is a little easier to get through than that, but is just as valuable.

Why me?

I started my professional career as a marketing consultant before I had even left college.

My first client was a little "mom and pop" store in a local strip plaza. They ran a business called "Allied Services", which was a forerunner to Mailboxes, Etc, (which has now become the UPS Store). Unfortunately, they were way ahead of their time. It was 1984, and they needed people to come into their store so they could explain their great services: packing, shipping and mailbox rentals. It doesn't take an MBA in marketing to realize their business name was a major handicap.

"Allied Services" means absolutely nothing, but it was the franchise name, and so they were stuck with it. But I liked these people, as they embodied one of my key business philosophies:

When life gives you lemons, start the Tropicana Corporation

They made a strategic decision to utilize their retail storefront to their advantage. In 1984, video rentals were just taking off. Local VHS rental stores had huge annual membership fees (some in excess of $750 a year), plus it was $4.00 per night to rent a movie. In today's dollars, that's like paying $2000 to join and $10 a night for rentals. But we all did it, because at that time, a new VHS copy of Star Wars was $129.00. Just six movie purchases paid for your annual membership, and that is how those early video stores positioned themselves.

Allied Services, however, was not exclusively a video store. Their other shipping business just barely paid the bills, so aside from the cost of the movies, they could rent them for whatever they chose. And they chose very well. Their rental rate was $2.00 per night. And they had NO membership fee. Period. Zero. Nada. Zip.

And their shelves sat full of movies, night after night, week after week. That's where I came in.

I first noticed the tiny ad the owners placed in the campus newspaper every Thursday. Of course, you will immediately see the classic mistake all business owners make, as I reproduce their regular ad for you here:

Besides the obvious mistake of leading with a name that says absolutely nothing about their product line, the ad simply lacked the kick it needed. This ad, however, with just a few improvements, could deliver the "search" results the owners wanted. Here's what I did with the ad:

1^{99}

MOVIE RENTALS
NO membership fee!

Allied Services
Next to
Shaw's Grocery Store
Durham Plaza

The ad appeared on a Thursday morning. I stopped by the store after classes late that afternoon. The first thing I noticed was that there was really nobody in the store. My heart sank. Then, on opening the door, I noticed something else.

Not only were there no customers in the store… but there were no MOVIES in the store.

The shelves were almost completely empty. There were only a handful of movies left, spread across four 16-foot shelves, but for all intents and purposes, they were empty. Bare. Picked clean.

And the owner looked up from the counter, saw it was me, and ran around the counter to shake my hand. He then told me that when he had arrived to open the store at 10:00 that morning, there was a line down the sidewalk. People were carrying the newspaper, opened to the page his ad was on. When he let them in, people were pointing to the ad, as if it were a coupon, and saying, "I want this deal!" From the consumers perspective, the deal bordered on incredulous. People could barely believe it. They thought it must be a one day sale, or that it had caveats and limitations as to which movies, and by God they were going to get their pound of flesh because those limits weren't expressed in the ad and so they didn't apply to people carrying the ad. His shelves were bare, his floor traffic increased geometrically, and eventually his mailbox rentals and shipping business took off, just as he had hoped.

And so did my love for marketing. I was hooked. I had helped someone become a successful, independent business owner. I had assisted someone in achieving the American dream of owning his own business, setting his own rules, earning exactly what he was worth, and living the life he wanted to live.

I left college and became the Director of Marketing for an eleven-state agricultural co-op. Not many people walked out of class one day, and into a company car the very next. From there I went on to doing consulting jobs for television stations, educational course providers, and lots and lots of small businesses that wanted to be big businesses.

And then came the internet.

I was busy inventing products, working in classic channels of marketing, and selling to consumers. The idea of business marketing online really wasn't on my radar screen. In 2010, I still didn't have a Facebook account, and I was entirely invisible on Linked In. But that all changed when a consulting client brought me on board to "figure out" internet marketing. He had several products he had invented, or was ready to bring to market from other countries, but nothing he could find showed him a system for successfully marketing those various products on line. I had a good track record for analyzing complex systems, from marketing, to financial markets, to ancient belief systems, to advertising algorithms, but I had never really turned my attention to the internet.

When he hired my agency, I found a whole new dictionary of terms, a new set of rules, and a completely different media concept... but there was something strangely familiar about all of it. Like Champollion, who in 1822 first translated ancient Egyptian hieroglyphs by studying the Rosetta Stone, I could see something ghostlike and parallel to the world of marketing I had been using and teaching for 25 years, but somehow it was different. And then, like Champollion did when he realized the symbols in the ovals represented the names of kings, I found the key. The first step forward was in learning about social media. By then I had created multiple Facebook pages for clients and was running them just like everybody else. I was using the Fan pages to announce product sales, special events, discounts and deals. Response was mediocre, regardless of the "deal" being put forth in the ad. Unlike the Allied Services marketing concept, the "$1.99 Movie Rental" just didn't have the punch it should have had. That's when I employed another one of my business philosophies:

Step back. Move up a level. Change the rules.

When I started scanning all the best, most effective Social Media marketing campaigns, I noticed that they didn't appear to be campaigns at all. It was the name of that area of online marketing that finally hit me.

The key to social media isn't "media"; it's "social".

Being sincerely social was how you became successful on the internet. The fact is, if you wanted real people to come to your real business and spend real money, then you had to be a real person, engaging with other real people. What a simple truth, but one that, to this day, still escapes most small business owners. When you talk about communicating on the web, many people think of the internet trolls who textually accost people on message boards and blogs. The internet is a place where anonymity rules. But trolls never sell anything, and anonymous people really can't buy your product. They have to have a credit card. The internet was quickly becoming the new "town square", where people met, talked, traded stories of happiness and horror, and generally made the world a better place by sharing. This is where they would post bulletins about upcoming concerts in the park, or hand out flyers to people passing by letting them know that there is a sale tomorrow at the hardware store.

The internet wasn't about an anonymous world. It was about a global community, made up of real people with real profiles and real families and real stories and real faces. It wasn't about putting a billboard up on the highway, or creating a funny mascot for your car dealership. It was about the business owner, and what he or she felt was important in how they run their businesses. It was about how they honestly interacted with the customers. The days of hiding one's business practices were over. You could no longer be that plumber that ripped people off. Thanks to Angie's list, and then social media, that became a virtual impossibility. Everybody can know about you now.

And is that a lot more work?

It sure can be, if you don't have a system in place to manage it. That's where I really started digging in. I began looking at SEO (Search Engine Optimization), and analyzing the Google algorithms, and all the anecdotal stories I heard. There is an element of truth in every piece of anecdotal evidence. The key is finding the breadcrumbs that eventually construct the theory that holds those clues together.

As I dug deeper, I discovered that all the best, foundational online business marketing fit into five categories of activity. Any one of these categories would yield results, but you couldn't get that "spark" of ignition without engaging in at least these five areas. These five areas, or Five Drivers, as I called them, all built on each other, and drove results higher by working together. So, what are these "Five Drivers"?

- SRO (Search Result Optimization)

- Site Design

- Social Media

- Email

- Multi-Media

When a company was utilizing all five of these drivers for its online marketing, it created a regular flow of prospects, leads and sales. As I said before, any one of these can work well if done right, but all five together seemed to create what I can only describe as a "fusion reaction", whereby the system fueled itself, causing its own output to increase beyond the sum of the five individual parts.

For big companies, it wasn't a hard sell to tell them they needed five departments within their marketing division to handle these areas of expertise. After all, they were accustomed to having specialists for buying print space in newspapers, versus those who negotiated the rates on multiple market ten second traffic report sponsorships. But until now, "online marketing" was considered to be one big lump that might have been assigned one person, or one small team. But the people who are good at crafting a brand image for a YouTube video aren't necessarily the same people you want creating your meta tags and internal link structures for a blog article.

The good news is, the big business's ability to hire five marketing specialists is also their weakness, compared to you, the small business owner. You know your business. You know what's happening just about every minute of every day. You know your customers, and you know what they like to hear just before they buy from you. Teaching that to a marketing employee takes about 600 hours of training, on site visits, and at least two corporate retreats to Las Vegas. As a small business owner and entrepreneur, you are precisely in the sweet spot. But you need to learn one more lesson before we get to some even better news about the Five Drivers program:

All business is marketing

I can't stress that simple phrase nearly enough. It doesn't matter how efficient your delivery system is; how gorgeous your displays are; how low your prices are compared to the competition. If you don't have customers, you don't have a business. And marketing is the ONLY way to get customers. It is your business. Finding customers is your business. Period. You can always change what you sell them, but if you don't have them, you can't sell them anything.

If you can accept that, then I'm going to have you take a step even further down this rabbit hole.

Businesses exist inside a marketplace. Sometimes it's a flea market. Sometimes it's a supermarket plaza. Sometimes it's a global marketplace. It's a market, regardless of where your business is located, finds customers, or makes sales. Every part of your business is part of that market. When you bring your products in to sell, that's part of marketing, because you have to decide which products to purchase, which ingredients you will procure, or which packaging you choose. Then you put the products into a display of some sort. That display could be the shelves in your store, the pages on your website, or into boxes for resale. Then the customers receive the product, and put it to use.

Every single step of that process is informed by the market. From your choice of ingredients, to the choice of colors in your logo, to the choice of packaging when you turn over the final product to the final consumer, is all informed by your knowledge of the market. That's *marketing*. Knowing what ingredients your customers prefer, knowing how to communicate your business's commitment to its style of product by rendering a logo that communicates that commitment, and then displaying and delivering that product in a way that satisfies those customers... it's all marketing. So get good at it.

The First Driver

SRO
SRO: Search Result Optimization

First of all, let's get the fancy acronyms out of the way. SEO just stands for "Search Engine Optimization". It refers to the task of making your site easily "findable" (or indexed) by a search engine like Google, Bing, Yahoo or DuckDuckGo. You do this one time, when you are first building your website. It's like giving the search engines a key to the back door so they can come visit any time they want to see what's new or different in your "house". Search Result Optimization, however, is a verb. SRO is the actual result you achieve from SEO. Your goal is to get as close to the first listing on a SERP (Search Engine Result Page) as you can. Good SRO can do that for you.

To begin with, we have to establish the fact that the internet is a HUGE place, where almost NOBODY has ever heard of you, your business, or your service. It never ceases to amaze me how many people think they've scored a major SRO victory because when you look up their business name in Google, their website shows up somewhere on the first page.

That's not a victory, folks. That's about as hard to do as standing on the tracks and getting hit by a train.

The real purpose of internet marketing is not to be easily found by people who already know about you (although that has its proper place, and we'll talk about that in the chapter on Site Design), but rather to help people who are searching for your product or service to discover that you exist.

Granted, there are a few older, well established businesses who have spent tens of thousands, even hundreds of thousands of dollars on print and broadcast advertising over the years, and for them they believe their primary goal is to "locate" the people who already know they exist. The fact is, in my forty years of marketing, I can tell you that humans simply don't respond that way.

For example, here's a challenge for you. Name the nearest Ford dealership to you. Then try GMC, Chevy, Dodge, Nissan, Hyundai, Kia and Lexus. Odds are, you are very familiar with one (probably the last place you bought a car), and you know WHERE the others are, but you don't actually know the name of the dealership. So, if you've decided you want to change from Kia to Nissan, you will run a search for a Nissan dealership in your town, i.e. "Nissan dealer Manchester NH". Seems perfectly reasonable, right? It should be easy. In fact, how can there really be more than ONE result?

Let's take a look at what Google ACTUALLY turns up as a response. Here's the first page, after the ads:

Nissan Dealership -Team Nissan, Manchester -Serving ...
www.teamnissannh.com/ ▾
Team Nissan of Manchester NH is one of the best new and used car dealers in NH.
Team Nissan has a wide selection of Nissan vehicles in Manchester NH plus ...
Pre-Owned Inventory - Pre-Owned Specials - Service - New Inventory

Team Nissan Used Nissan Car, Truck, SUV Dealer ...
www.teamnissannh.com/used-inventory/index.htm ▾
Team Nissan carries a variety of Certified Pre-Owned used cars in Nashua, NH ...

New Hampshire Team Nissan Dealer Manchester NH | Find...
www.teamnissannh.com/new-inventory/index.htm ▾
Team Nissan is one of the top Nissan dealers in NH for new and used Nissan ..

Nissan Dealers In New Hampshire | Nissan USA
www.nissanusa.com/nissandealers/.../new-hampshi... ▾ Nissan Motor Co., Ltd. ▾
Nissan USA Official Site: Use the dealer locator to find local Nissan dealers in New
Hampshire. .... 70 KELLER ST. MANCHESTER, NH 03103. 603-644-8326.

Concord Nissan | New Nissan dealership in Concord, NH ...
www.concordnissan.com/ ▾ Concord Nissan ▾
We are NEW and improved at the same location on 175 Manchester st in Concord New
Hampshire- Concord NH Nissan Dealer. We are off of Exit 13 off of 93 .

Nissan Dealership Keene, Lebanon NH | New & Used Cars ...
www.teamnissannorth.com/ ▾
Team Nissan North in Lebanon, NH is one of the best new and used car dealers serving
... Our Manchester location is the largest volume dealer in the tri-state ...

Find Nissan Dealers in Manchester, New Hampshire
www.edmunds.com › ... › Hillsborough County ▾ Edmunds.com ▾
Edmunds.com can get you started on the right track with a convenient directory of
Nissan car dealerships in and around Manchester, New Hampshire. Compare ...

But here's the really important part:

See that? Over 120,000 results come up for this search.

So, unless you've spent a LOT of money making SURE that when people search for those words, words

20

that seem so obvious and simple that they can't miss, you are likely to get pushed WAY down the pages when people who know you are there are trying to find you.

Starting to get the picture?

What is SRO?

As I said above, SRO is the Search Result Optimization. In order to be found on the internet, you have to be crystal clear about who you are, or more appropriately, "who" your business is. This clarity of description is vital, as the average American is being pummeled by media messages every minute they are awake. When I started my career in marketing, the typical American was seeing over 600 marketing messages a day. That was almost one message every ten minutes. This was an outrageously high number, and we were wondering then how we could get our message seen or heard.

Today, the number exceeds 3,000, with some estimates as high as 5,000. That means your brain is absorbing an advertising message from somebody at least every FIVE SECONDS. Some of these "messages" that advertisers are paying for consumers to absorb are 30 seconds long. To trap someone's attention for half a minute, the consumer has to decide to ignore five other messages they could be viewing instead of yours.

That is some serious competition. And that is why big businesses have big advertising budgets and massive creative budgets, working 24/7 to design marketing messages that directly appeal to their target audience.

But you're reading this book, and this book wasn't written for them.

It was written for you.

So, now that I've completely destroyed your dreams of massive fame, with your product becoming a household name like Whirlpool, Apple or Tesla, let's start talking about how you can still succeed at building the successful business of your dreams.

> **IMPORTANT: Please realize that this is not a sprint, it is a *marathon*. There is no shortcut to long term success, especially when it comes to online marketing. I know this is exactly the opposite of what you hear, but the fact is, that myth was created during the "Wild West" days of the internet, when there weren't so many sites, and consumers weren't as adept as they are today in finding the USEFUL information they desire. It is a slow haul becoming the trusted source for information, so you have to be consistent and persistent in creating your content.**

There's an old saying in marketing, and it goes something like this:

> *"People don't want to buy a drill. They want to buy a hole."*

When people finally get their brains wrapped around that simple axiom, their businesses can begin to market properly. Let me take it a bit further by giving industry examples from my own coaching and consulting clients.

- You're not selling insurance policies. You're providing peace of mind and a sense of security.

- You're not selling an exercise device. You're selling good posture and a long, healthy life.

- You're not selling yourself as a graduate of an Ivy League business school. You're selling the HR manager on the fact that he will have all the necessary justifications and support documentation for explaining to his boss about why you were obviously the best choice for the job, even though you failed. (The vast majority of HR people are only worried about justifying their decisions when they go wrong, and NOT about finding the best candidate for the job. Generally, they get little or no credit for finding the right people, but all the blame for hiring the wrong one).

And that brings us to a very important point in SRO:

You have to know what your prospective customers are THINKING!

The good news is, mindreading has never been easier.

Know Your Prospect

Remember the old days when you would go to the mall and see people loitering around one particular section, clipboards in hand, waiting to pounce on anyone who makes eye contact? Those people were $8 an hour "surveyors". They were paid to ask you a list of questions, based on your physical appearance. In other words, their clients may be looking for women between the ages of 30 and 50, so they would try to engage anybody that fit that description, in hopes that some of them would take a few minutes to answer their questions.

That's how marketing research USED to be done. It was expensive. It was slow. And surprisingly, it was not very reliable.

In today's world, what we have found out is that people ask a lot of questions. Fortunately, they ask most of them in one place, typing them into a little white box, and then pressing "Search".

And, as luck would have it, this question-gathering-device has an amazingly good memory.

If you understand anything about survey psychology, you know that there is a real challenge in getting people to answer your questions in an honest, helpful fashion. It's not that people are being intentionally dishonest, but rather the very act of asking THEM a question can create a substantial level of error in the results. For example, if I ask you this question, let's see what your answer is:

What brand of car do you think you'll buy next:

A. Ford

B. Chrysler

C. Chevy

D. Lexus

E. Other

You will be artificially forcing them to choose from your finite list, the featured auto manufacturers on the list may cause people to "remember" something they liked about a Ford, but not recall a feature in a Honda that will eventually sway their decision, and frankly, you will end up talking to people who may not be planning on buying a new car ever.

But what if you could get the questions *they* were asking? What if you could see their *real* thoughts or ideas on car buying, brands, features and prices that they wouldn't otherwise tell you? Just how useful would that information be?

Yes. That's where the real power of search engine data comes into play. That's why it is crucial that we understand how to find, interpret and use keywords to your business's advantage. When you eventually grasp the real power of key words, you will see not only your own business in a new light, but you may also see businesses you could be doing right now, that you never knew existed.

The Secret to Key Words

Key words are what people type into a search engine to find their results. The results show up on what are called "SERPs", or "Search Engine Results Pages". (Not terribly clever, I know, but the internet wasn't invented by a bunch of creative marketing geniuses.) A page one SERP is the best possible outcome of a good SRO strategy. You will be on the first page people find when they look for your product or service. The closer you are to the first position (directly under the paid ads), the better your clickthrough rate will be. To put this in perspective, remember that even as far back as of 2011, 94% of the search audience never even clicked on "Next page". They ONLY clicked on the first page links, and of those, the first organic link on the page (the ones that are NOT paid advertising) got 53% of the clicks. So, this is definitely the only place to be if you want to win at marketing your business on the internet. And today it's only worse.

Most business owners think that the only choice they have is to find their key words, and then go out and fight for the placement they deserve. But remember what I just said: if you're not on page one, you're wasting your time. To understand placement, we have to understand what general factors Google uses to decide "who's on first". To understand that, we have to start using some technical lingo that sounds scary, but is really pretty simple.

The Google Algorithm – No knowledge of advanced mathematics required (Phew!)

Google is a giant repository of information on all of the significant websites on the planet. When you "Google" something, contrary to popular belief, you aren't actually looking at the whole internet trying to find your results. Think about it. How long do you sit and wait for some websites to load, so that you can see if it really is what you're looking for? Can you imagine how slow a Google search would be if you had to wait for every site to "load" so it could be searched for you? If you recall, in our previous example we had over 120,000 results come up for Nissan dealerships in Manchester, NH. Imagine how many HOURS it would take to load over a hundred thousand websites, scan their pages, and then get back to you with the results.

Google solved that problem (as did every other search engine) by creating its own private database of all websites on the net. So instead of searching the entire internet every time, all it has to do is search ONE giant database that they host on their own servers. They have reduced the internet to one, incredibly huge Excel spreadsheet, basically. Once it's all put in one location, then searching that ONE spreadsheet for the information you want is infinitely faster.

But what difference does that make to you? A lot, actually.

This means that regardless of what you do on your website today, your customers, or prospective customers, will not be able to search for that change until Google decides to scan your website and store that new information in its massive database. Only what is stored in that database can be searched. This is a very important distinction, and helps us to understand how we can get our arms around the Google algorithm and use it to our advantage.

What's an Algorithm?

Simply put, an algorithm is nothing but a formula that you create and it does what you want it to do. It's not exactly a program, as a program runs a computer. An algorithm doesn't require a program, as it is a formula that is always applied. A simple algorithm we all know is the algorithm for figuring out the area of a rectangle: length times width. Whatever figures you pop into those two slots will always give you the area of a rectangle.

With Google, however, you are dealing with hundreds, even thousands of variables that have been programmed into the equations. These variables exist for one reason only: to FIND websites that relate to the search, and then to ELIMINATE all websites that are trying to game the system. Let's start by looking at some simple concepts, and how they relate to search engine results.

28

CASE STUDY: Tom's Bicycle Store

Tom sells bicycles. He creates a website that says he sells bicycles. You search for a store that sells bicycles. You find Tom's Bicycle Store.

That's the basic idea, anyway. It's the variables that now creep in and make SRO challenging.

First, if I'm in Kentucky, I'd probably like a bike seller in Kentucky. But I didn't say that in my search, so I will get 700,000 bicycle sellers from all over the world. I needed to narrow that down in order to find Tom's Bicycle Store. But did I mean new bikes or used bikes? Did I mean mountain bikes, touring bikes, e-bikes, or motor bikes? When you get your search terms right, Google will give you the results you really wanted.

So, as a customer, I have to be somewhat smart in how I search. But even then, there's the issue of Black Hat SEO sites. Black Hat SEO is what it is called when you use the search algorithm to lure people into your website, then try to sell them something they don't want at all. Imagine a storefront that had bikes in the windows, bikes in the name, and was called "Bill's Bike Store". Seems like just the right place if you're looking for bikes, right? Wrong. Inside Bill's Bike Store we actually find credit card applications. Lots of them. Everywhere. Because, really, Bill works for a credit card company and gets paid by the application. He doesn't care HOW you manage to arrive; he only cares that maybe you will fill out one of his applications. Some people actually think they're applying to buy a bike. Bill doesn't care. He's getting paid by the application. Getting paid matters to him. Your satisfaction with the search results is entirely outside of his field of vision.

That's where the OTHER side of the Google algorithm comes in. Google hunts Bill's site, notes he's advertising himself as a bike store, but then notices that he has no bikes for sale. He has no information on biking, tires, seats, or even pedals. Worse, he has just as much stuff on his site for horseback riding, dental implants, and online dating. And, to top it off, the domain name, "BillsSuperDiscountBikeStore.com" is actually only six months old. Google punishes people who do this, as Google's only concern is just the opposite of Bill's: they WANT you to be happy with your search results, otherwise you will use another search engine next time, and they won't be able to show you the paid ads they have on the SERP pages. That point bears restating: **Google is ONLY concerned with giving you the BEST results based on your search, because that is how they keep you logging back into Google the next time you have a question.**

And that point is the biggest clue in how you can use the Google Algorithm to successfully advertise your small business on the internet. Let's dig in to how that actually works.

Forget about what you do

I know. I just told you that you have to absolutely be honest about what you do. But, in order for your online marketing to work, you have to stop thinking that you know what you do, and start considering that you might be the solution to a problem you didn't know people were having. One of the best ways to understand how to get around the battle for page one is... to fight for a different page one.

You see, just because Tom sells bikes doesn't mean that "bikes for sale" is the best thing for Tom to target with his website. With a little homework, you can discover certain terms that are being searched, but DON'T have sixty thousand people trying to fight for page one. Because, really, do you need sixty-thousand new leads every month to stay in business? Probably not. In fact, If you just had sixty... or even six... you'd probably be able to make a good go of your business. So start to think in terms of what you need, and not necessarily what is out there to be had.

Let's actually run some analyses to see what the difference is between Tom trying to target "bicycle" from his store in Topeka, Kansas.

My software tells me that today there are approximately (get ready for it) 1,500,000 searches for the word "bicycle" ... PER MONTH! Wow! Isn't that fantastic? If Tom can just get one out of 10,000 searches to go his way, he'll have an extra 150 sales per month! He'll be able to open a second store, hire help, and even give bikes to charities!

So this becomes Tom's quest. He puts the word "bicycle" into his website everywhere he can. He creates pages with just the name "bicycle" in it. And, after three months of intensive blogging to create backlinks, lots of reviews written on line, super loyal customers on social media sharing his content everywhere, he checks and sees that he is not only "off" page one (death), but he is somewhere back on page 86, right under an article from CNN about how a bicycle was stolen from a Hollywood actor on vacation in Bermuda. Tom has spent hundreds of hours, and maybe even thousands of dollars, trying to get his share of the 1.5 million searches, and has come up entirely empty handed.

But what if Tom had started just a little differently?

Software exists today that can reverse Google's algorithm on itself, and not only run the search you request, but also create variations in the search. So, in this real life example, let's see what happens if we make just a simple adjustment, and go from a keyword, to what is called a "long tail keyword". Or, in English, we're going to search for a phrase instead of a word.

What if we changed the search term from "bicycle" to "bicycles Topeka"? Well, we would certainly have a LOT fewer searches to deal with. In fact, according to my software, there are exactly ZERO searches per month for bicycles in Topeka. It could be that Tom started his bicycle store in a really bad location. But surely there are a lot of people who still want to buy bicycles, and might even buy them online, right?

Very right.

If you change the words again, but this time to "bicycle for sale", you end up getting 22,200 searches per month. The key with this phrase, however, is that NOBODY on the first three Google SERPs is actually targeting it with their websites! This long tail keyword has no competition from any of the top Google results. Google WANTS to find the best results, but the top results aren't always good results. Let's repeat that:

The top results aren't always good results.

This is your magic spell for getting business from online marketing. If there's one phrase that you need to learn about SRO marketing, it's this one: If you can create results that actually SATISFY the Google algorithm's appetite for what it thinks is a quality result, then you can move really fast toward that coveted "Page One" position. Now, this is a real life example of a search I ran several years ago. Obviously by the time you read this, I hope somebody will probably have capitalized on this weakness, so don't bother trying to open an online bike store based on this advice. And for goodness sake, don't use it to attract people to your credit card application site! Here's what will happen if you do:

You will get Sandboxed.

When Google finds a site that is either too new, too generic, or too dishonest, they immediately "sandbox" that website. Let's handle those in reverse order.

Too Dishonest: Your site isn't what you say it is. You have created a string of phony backlinks and gibberish AI written articles on the web with spammy text surrounding your connection back to your site (that's a backlink, by the way). Google has gotten amazingly good at detecting these Black Hat methods, and will put your website into a penalty box, or "sandbox" if you are caught using them. If you are really a fraud trying to redirect traffic where it doesn't belong, Google will be as merciless as you are dishonest. Shame on you, and don't come back.

Too Generic: If Google can't figure out what you're selling, they won't put you anywhere. You're not even really "sandboxed"… you're just ignored. Would you believe that this is the category that MOST websites actually fall into? According to the example above, NOBODY has optimized their website for the key phrase "bicycle for sale", but you can still see that over 45 MILLION results come up. Why is that? Because Google is trying hard to deliver SOMETHING to the searcher, so it is using its database to deliver the "next best thing". It sends you to Dick's Sporting Goods, Amazon, Walmart and Ebay. If you think about it, if you are bicycle shopping in Kansas, you already KNOW about those options. You were looking for something a little more personal. You wanted advice, expertise, and not an automated callbox at the end of the aisle that shouts over the intercom, "Customer waiting in the Outdoor Sport Department"! But I can tell you that months after I first published this not one single major bicycle shop has gone online and targeted these words in any effective manner. In fact, when I scan down the page, here is the first "private" bicycle store, and here is what they have for their key targeting words:

Description: Great selection of 29ers, full suspension and women's mountain bikes

Keywords: Mountain bikes, Mongoose mountain bike, Schwinn mountain bike, full suspension mountain bike, GT mountain bike, 26 mountain bike, mountain bike suspension, women's mountain bike, 20 mountain bike, Diamondback mountain bike, mountain bike sale

Google had to SETTLE for these people as an answer to over twenty-thousand searches per month. But what if you knew that nobody was targeting perfectly good words that describe your business, and even if it meant you gave up going after the big one, you could actually start to get the results you need from your SRO efforts?

That makes SRO worth it. That's what you need to do with your website if you're going to succeed at business marketing online. Once you understand that, we can then move on to the "how".

Creating your Gravity Well

Have you ever seen a depiction of the way gravity works, perhaps on a documentary on the planets, or back in science class? Here's a quick recap.

Picture "space" as a big rubber sheet. Now, picture Earth as a bowling ball being placed on that big sheet of rubber. Here's an image to help you see what would happen.

Now imagine rolling a marble across the sheet. It would be diverted by the dip in the sheet created by the Earth. The ball is creating what is called a "gravity well", a place that attracts objects, like the marble, within its vicinity. Naturally, this is not how gravity "really" works, but it serves the purpose of explaining the way things are attracted to objects with mass, and how that mass affects the space around it.

Your website is the planet on the sheet. The sheet is the internet. Your customers are the marbles. Your job is to take your website and make the biggest dent you can in the internet, so that you don't lose your marbles.

Make sense?

Google has very specific ideas of what things add to your mass, and thus count in the creation of your gravity well. Let's examine those pieces, one at a time.

Fresh Content

One of the most important elements of the all search engine algorithms is the "freshness" of your content. Search engines think an old site is great, but not if the content hasn't changed in eight months. There is a massive amount of new information available on the internet, and search engines don't want to send their valuable customers to a site that doesn't look like it is regularly updated to reflect recent changes in a field, even if there haven't been any recent changes in that field. Face it, the Pythagorean Theorem hasn't changed much in 2000 years, but a site that posted an explanation five years ago is going to get pummeled in the search results by a site that has a new articles about how the Pythagorean Theorem is being taught in various ways in schools this year. Search engines are in the business of sending their customers to the sites that deliver the most relevant, satisfying content. If their customers aren't satisfied, they'll just try another search engine.

So, it's your job to keep your website regularly updated with new, relevant content. That does NOT mean you update your front page to reflect your summer vacation hours, or that you just change the pictures. Search engines don't really care about pictures, except in specific circumstances we will discuss later in the section on media.

The good thing is, content is something you can control. If you have a well designed site, it will be easy for your to update this content quickly and easily yourself.

Author's Note: The following section is really designed for people who are selling products online. If you are not intending to have an online store where you are competing for SRO-based customers, I suggest you just give it a quick skim and move onto the next part of the book. - APS

Meta Tags

When a sheriff is looking at a line of cars in front of him at a light, he really doesn't have any special way of knowing which car belongs to whom, unless he has some kind of special tool to tell him quickly who owns the car, when it was registered, and whether or not it has insurance on it. That one tool the sheriff uses is the license plate. In the south, license plates are actually called "tags", so the metaphor works even better. Like your tag on your car, Google uses your site tags to quickly and easily identify the subject matter of your site and categorize it accordingly. There are a few myths about meta tags that we need to dispel, but overall, they are pretty simple and easy to understand, and as long as you are using them right, you can, at the very least, get ranked under your business name in the SERPs.

Title Tag:

The title tag of your site is crucial to being found by search engines. In fact, it may be one of the most important functions available... and it is the most commonly messed up by business owners. There are two parts to a title tag, and you should get comfortable in handling them both. One part is the part at the beginning that is easily visible to the customer/user when they first access your site. It is that word or words that appear in the browser window tab. For example, when you go to WholeFoods.com, you see "Whole Foods...." In your browser tab, or a part of it, depending upon how many tabs you have open. It is good to have a message that clearly identifies the site as the one they think they are supposed to be on, so be sure to have your company name (or website name) right at the beginning. That's the first part of the title tag.

The second part of the title tag is what comes AFTER the easily visible part. Many websites use the "|" symbol to split the name into two parts. It's the part AFTER that symbol that works phenomenally well for SRO purposes, and doesn't mess up your branding in the least. If you hover over the tab for Whole Foods, you will see the full title tag actually reads, "Whole Foods Market | Whole Foods Market". That's their home page, so they want to make sure that Google sees that business name reflected in their page title. When Google is hunting for pages, it will first look for a relevant page title that matches the search. Doesn't that just make sense? It's like the sheriff being on the lookout for a car with Georgia tags. The letters and numbers don't make much difference if it's not a Georgia tag, so he's going to look for peaches on the plate.

If you click on a link on the Whole Foods site, however, you will discover that the title tags change. Instead of "Whole Foods Market | Whole Foods Market", you see something like "Healthy Eating | Whole Foods Market". My personal opinion is that for small businesses with less custom branding in their sites, it is probably better to make sure your site visitors are sure they haven't left your site. The point is, this particular feature of a website can look absolutely consistent to your site visitors, but at the same time allow you to use your SRO key words where they matter most.

Getting back to our bike shop example, the page title for the home page should probably read, "Tom's Bicycle Store | Bicycle for Sale". Of course, I am assuming that Tom will actually have a bicycle for sale on his home page... preferably several. If not, then he should reserve that particular title tag for a page where people will land and find the bicycles he has for sale. Remember, your home page does not have to be the first page every visitor sees. Get over the idea that everybody will come to your site through the front door. Every page needs to be designed so that it engages visitors and moves them through your Desired Site Process (DSP).

Get over the idea that everybody will come to your site through the front door. Every page needs to be designed so that it engages visitors and moves them through your Desired Site Process (DSP).

Don't cram this title tag with every key word you think you want. Keep it simple, and get into the habit of changing the title tags to match specific pages. If you have new and used bikes, for example, don't put "Tom's Bicycle Store | New and Used Bicycles for Sale" as the title. Google prefers exact phrase matches FIRST, and the title listed above will NOT give a high ranking for "New Bicycles for Sale", because that isn't what it says. "Used bicycles for sale" will come up, but not until it stumbles past the "New and" part. So, break your bikes up into two categories, and show them on separate pages with one page titled "New Bicycles for Sale" and the other "Used Bicycles for Sale".

Meta Description

The meta description tag used to be a lot more important than it is now, thanks to the introduction of rich snippets. The description was the piece of text that Google would capture and display when generating your search result, if it contained the appropriate key words. That's why it is important to make sure your meta description is written more as a sales pitch for your product, rather than cramming it with key words. Let's step away from bicycles for a second, and focus on Viterium Face Cream, a fictional anti-wrinkle product. The key phrase "wrinkle removal" gets over 5000 searches a month, but there is heavy competition for that in the top three pages of Google SERPs. Instead, our software shows us that a one-off phrase, "best anti aging products" has nobody competing for it with their SRO design, and is actually generating an average of 8100 searches per month. Bingo! That's our target. But here is an example of how NOT to target your target:

Meta Description: the best anti aging products is viterium anti aging products face cream because viterium is the best anti aging products for people looking for anti aging products. Viterium.

You've seen stuff like that show up on Google, and what's YOUR first thought? It's a scam page, designed to mislead me into clicking on the link and seeing their line of driveway paving chemicals, or worse, there's a virus on the page and by clicking on such an obvious scam, I'll actually hurt my computer.

Instead, here is a better suggestion for a better description:

Meta Description: Compared to the best anti aging products , Viterium ™ was found to perform better, faster, and with fewer adverse side effects

because it is made with only natural ingredients. Shop Viterium.com for the lowest price on Viterium.

Think about what that will look like when it shows up in the SERP results. It's your place to build your key words right into your sales pitch. Please note that I intentionally left a space after the word "products", and before the comma. This is not a typo. I don't want Google to have to "think" about whether the punctuation belongs as part of the search or not. I'm giving them a clean phrase to find, and then letting them decide whether they approve of my grammar or not. There is a school of thought that says Google ignores punctuation. My thought is, better safe than sorry.

Now, I've been talking about the meta description tag as if it still mattered. To a certain extent, it still does, but in 2014, Google (and subsequently the other major search engines) followed the new path of the "Rich Snippet". Everything you're learning about the Description Tag also applies to Rich Snippets, but the Rich Snippet allows you a new way to organize your individual products, pages or articles so that Google recognizes them for what you want them to be. You still have to have your description tags in place, but you need to repeat them specifically for search engine optimization. We'll get into that in the chapter on Site Design.

Key Word Tag

Key words were the hotspot for stuffing tags that you hoped Google would see and index. Not any more, except in certain circumstances. Many books, videos and gurus will tell you to just skip on the key word meta tags these days, because Google virtually ignores them, and they are only used internally by your current users for searches within your site. (For example, somebody comes to your Accountant website to see if you handle IRS Audits, so they do a word search from your home page for "IRS Audits". If you have that in your tags, it will direct them to the pages that contain that tag.)

However, there is a qualifier for this particular exclusion of key word tags, and it specifically says that Google is ignoring them for highly competitive words. The fact is, our strategy for organic SRO means we are intentionally targeting LOW competition words. Therefore, Google may take a liking to a site that has its name, description and tags coordinated to fit their exact desired search. So, in our case, we will be advising you to continue using the Key Word Tags, but use them wisely.

When constructing your key words, remember that Google is looking for an exact phrase match. This is the place where Google is most forgiving of "cramming". I suggest you start with your top key word or phrase, and then taper them off by value. However, your first key word should always be your product name. So, sticking with the example above, we would construct our key word list as follows:

Key Words: Viterium, best anti aging products, best anti aging serum, how to remove wrinkles, anti age cream

These key words have the following average monthly searches:

Best anti aging products   8,100

Best anti aging serum   3,600

How to remove wrinkles   1,600

Anti age cream   1,300

Those tags represent over 14,000 searches per month, and as of the date of writing this, there were few or no websites properly targeting those words. 14,000 clicks a month could launch a whole business, if the rest of the site is designed properly to convert clicks into sales.

Site Map
Your website will be a collection of a few, or perhaps several hundred pages. Google needs to know which ones YOU consider to be important enough to "crawl" (or scan, as humans would see it) and how often it should do so. That's why you give Google a site map.

The site map is a simple file called "sitemap.xml", and it exists right in the same folder as your homepage (index.html, index.htm, index.php, etc). Below is an example of a sitemap, and once you see it, you will understand why Google likes to find them where they belong.

URL	Priority	Change Frequency	LastChange (GMT)
http://www.extra.biz/blog/about-me/	100%	Monthly	2014-06-27 14:11
http://www.extra.biz/blog/disclaimer/	100%	Monthly	2013-12-19 23:23
http://www.extra.biz/blog/contact-me/	100%	Monthly	2015-12-22 01:49
http://www.extra.biz/blog/	100%	Monthly	2013-12-23 16:40
http://www.extra.biz/blog/newsletter/	100%	Monthly	2014-06-26 00:55
http://www.extra.biz/blog/laptop-repair/	100%	Monthly	2014-06-27 15:45
http://www.extra.biz/blog/pc-repair/	100%	Monthly	2014-08-28 05:09
http://www.extra.biz/blog/network-setup/	100%	Monthly	2014-08-27 14:28
http://www.extra.biz/blog/pc-tuneup/	100%	Monthly	2014-08-27 14:54
http://www.extra.biz/blog/videos-setting-up-parental-controls-in-windows/	100%	Monthly	2015-12-21 21:07
http://www.extra.biz/blog/fixing-a-slow-loading-computer/	100%	Monthly	2015-12-21 21:24
http://www.extra.biz/blog/videos-recording-custom-windows-8-lock-screen-on-pc/	100%	Monthly	2015-12-21 26:06

This sitemap is for a brand new project, so none of the customizations have hit the settings yet. But, from the list, you can see that the page priority (which pages Google should scan first if the robots only have a limited amount of time), the suggested return frequency for the robots, because that's how often you think you might be changing the content of pages, and the date of the last change to the page. Naturally, the column on the left is the direct URL link to the page in question.

If you look at your root folder, or public folder, and do NOT see a sitemap, you are basically surrendering a huge amount of tactical advantage to your competition. Don't do that. Generate the sitemap and be serious about what you ask Google to do with it. Don't make every page a 100% priority. Your "contact" page isn't going to change very much. It shouldn't be ranked equally with your "Latest News" page, which could change daily. Google also doesn't like being lied to. Never forget that.

For example, if you are writing one blog post per week, and that blog post appears dynamically[1] on your homepage, then you should tell the search engines to come back and rescan (recrawl) your home page at least once per week. The sitemap will automatically generate the new page (or at least it should if you're doing it right), and so Google will find your new article by virtue of its creation date. If this is a really important article, then giving it a 100% may be appropriate. If it's a story about a customer's dog that greeted you nicely, eh… not so much.

Rich Snippets

In the first issue of this book, Rich Snippets were the new thing in SRO, and all they were was a new form of identification for search engines so they can easily identify what your page is really about. The good news was, it takes a little more work to get them put together. The bad news is, Google is no longer weighing them heavily, and almost everybody is doing them. As usual, these were a gimmick that didn't really translate into more satisfied Search Engine Customers, so they ultimately because extra baggage on your page, and extra work for you that really wasn't returning anything of value.

I'm going to continue educating you on rich snippets, but only because they segue into a new kind of content

---

[1] This is for posts that do not appear on your homepage via an inline frame. Instead, the actual text shows up in your source code. More on this in site design.

that IS being utilized by Google, at least, to determine page ranking.

So, what is a rich snippet? The best way to understand it is by analogy. Imagine walking into an old fashioned library, and needing to find a book describing the trial of Socrates. It does no good to look for a book WRITTEN by Socrates, because (SPOILER ALERT!) not only did he die right after the trial, but Socrates never wrote anything himself! His students wrote everything we know of the man.

So, what do you do? Go to the section on Classics? Philosophy? Greek History? All of the above?

No. The first thing you do is go to the Card File. Those little three by five index cards contained everything, sorted by category, author or title. And that's the best part, because there just happens to be a book called "The Trial of Socrates", written by one of his students. Some guy named "Plato".

Rich Snippets are nothing but an index card that tells Google what's on your site. In fact, they look more like one of those index cards than you might think. Here's how one appears on a product page:

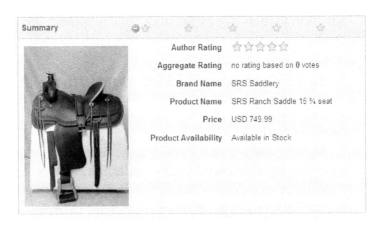

Like I said, it looks just like an index card, or maybe even a recipe card. As such, it is your recipe for success. Here's one from the same website, but this one is about an article they wrote on how to measure for a sidesaddle:

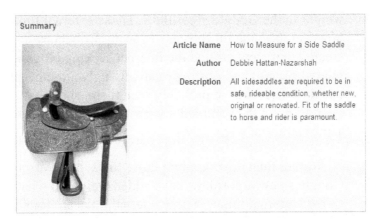

Summary	
Article Name	How to Measure for a Side Saddle
Author	Debbie Hattan-Nazarshah
Description	All sidesaddles are required to be in safe, rideable condition, whether new, original or renovated. Fit of the saddle to horse and rider is paramount.

What you see here is a great example of cross selling within a site. They have a reasonably expensive item that they want to sell, and they are using that item to attract attention to their site by creating content around the product.

Now, back to general SRO Marketing

Internal Links

Google used to heavily weigh the number of other websites that referenced your website. These were called "backlinks". Backlinks, traditionally, would show up in discussions, blogs, or on other pages built by web designers who wanted to reference other pages for their excellent content. So, for example, you are reading a site about bicycle parts, and you notice they have a link to Schwinn.com. That link to Schwinn's official website counts as a backlink for Schwinn.com, and because it is coming from a site that is all about bicycles, it carries weight in the Google algorithm[2]. Those external links, however, became far too easy to scam. Robots were created that went around the internet seeking blogs with related content and posting relatively ugly attempts at backlinking. You've probably seen them, showing up in the middle of the comments section on the New York Times editorial page.

Rather than downgrading those links, however, Google's new algorithms have added weight to what are called "internal links". These internal links are found

---

[2] Links from unrelated sites don't really help. A link to Schwinn from the wrinkle cream site probably isn't going to be counted by Google.

50

within the pages you create and control, and they make reference to other pages you create and control, within the same web site. This is another glorious gift from the Google gods, especially if you are just starting your site. You have the ability to cross reference between your own articles this way, adding more and more mass to your own "gravity well", simply by creating strong links between posts, pages and products. Let's see how this works by using a graphic representation of those kinds of links.

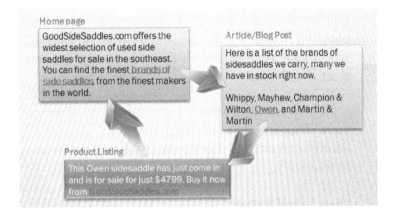

External SRO

Up to this point, all of this SRO work has been within your site. There is another important element of SERP rankings, and that is how you are viewed by the rest of your community. Search engines want to know what the rest of the world actually thinks of your site. If you are well liked and respected, they are more likely to refer their customers to you. (Sounds like regular face-to-face networking, doesn't it?) Search engines ascertain this by seeing how many other sites actually refer to your site, your articles, or your products. They also look closely at the quality and appropriateness of the links[3]. Here's an analogy for understanding backlinks. Think of them like business cards. If I find a stack of business cards on the counter at my doctor's office, they hold a certain level of respect, and I am going to overlay that air of dignity onto your business. If I find a stack of your business cards in the bathroom at a seedy, run-down gas station, I will probably make a point of avoiding your business at all costs. Backlinks work the same way. If you are the manufacturer of a medical device, then a backlink from sites like the Mayo Clinic or WebMD is worth a lot more to Google than one from a site that sells pirated software.

There are three areas where you can positively affect your SRO, and they are direct backlinks, directory listings and articles. Let's look at those three areas individually.

Direct Backlinks
Simply put, a direct backlink is a connection from one website to another. The quality of the "sending" site (the place where your link appears) directly affects how much mass this particular link adds to your gravity well. That connection actually transfers some of the importance and reputability of the sending site to your website. Naturally, there is little or nothing you can do

---

[3] Negative SEO is a tactic used by your competition that we will address a bit later.

about the reputation of someone else's site. They are what they are. A single backlink from a seedy site isn't going to negatively affect your SEO. Those things are considered "neutral", in the Google algorithm. Too many of them, and you'll have a problem. (This is where the concept of "negative SEO" comes into play). But if you have a good spread of links on decent sites that relate to your field, you won't have to concern yourself with the occasional outlier.

There are two elements to direct backlinks that we need to consider. One is how to get them, and the second is how they are constructed to give you maximum benefit.

There are basically three ways to get good backlinks. The first is through simply creating material that people want to quote, forward, or otherwise send their site visitors to you. One of the best ways to get high quality links of this nature is through direct contact and negotiation with the site creators/contributors at the major sites. Staying with our medical example, you can find a doctor or other specialist who contributes work to WebMD on a regular basis, and simply drop her an email to let her know about your product or service, so that she can keep it in mind when she writes her next article. There is a slightly (and by slightly, I mean "a lot") less kosher way of getting your backlinks onto big named websites, and that is through the posting abilities on the forums that follow the articles by these reputable authors. It is MUCH more advantageous to have your link contained directly in the body of the article than it is to have it in the comments section below. But, if you have tried and you can't break into the content itself, then there is no real downside to creating good content relating to the article in question, and then posting a link from the comments section of the forum back to your site, where people can read the rest of the article. Here is an example from a WebMD article that demonstrates this particular tactic.

7 Most Effective Exercises

http://www.webmd.com/fitness-exercise/guide/7-most-effective-exercises

4 years ago

 Andie_WebMD_Staff posted:

Experts say there is no magic to exercise: You get out of it what you put in. That doesn't mean you have to work out for hours each day. It just means you need to work smart.

That said, experts agree that not all exercises are created equal. Some are simply more efficient than others, whether they target multiple muscle groups, are suitable for a wide variety of fitness levels, or help you burn calories more effectively.

So what are the best exercises? We posed this question to four fitness experts and compiled a list of their favorites.

I bet you're surprised at the #1 exercise!

Do you agree? Was YOUR favorite exercise listed as one of the most effective? Share your tips, too.

A good response to this would be as follows:

"Andie,

The seven exercises they list are all excellent. I personally like planking, but this article seems to be a bit older than the planking craze. Would you put it on the list now? I'm a fitness trainer, and I have found that the people I counsel have trouble finding the time to exercise. Many of them do well with squats and walking, because they don't actually require workout clothes or a major disruption in the workplace. In fact, I developed a list of ten posture building exercises you can do at work. They include squats, walking, core exercises and some discreet stretches. You can see the whole list at http://www.2xmed.com/office-exercises.

Thanks for putting this article together. I'll be sure to pass it on to my clients! "

Notice the link is just provided for people who want MORE information about what I posted, and not as a way of redirecting people from what the author wrote. Think about it: you wouldn't want people to be drawn away from your article, but if someone is appearing to be an authority on a subject and is actually adding to your discussion, this makes for a great way to earn respectful backlinks. This is why I think services that sell you backlinks are going to eventually get you hurt in your SERP rankings. It won't take long before Google figures out how to discern between real backlinks and spam backlinks, so don't leave yourself exposed to the sandbox. Do it the right way the first time.

One of the thing that scares people about backlinking is that when you have the software to run the averages, you find that there is a tremendous difference between the average and the median number of backlinks on page one. Let me give you an hypothetical example. Your key word phrase is "lower back pain exercise". The software shows that the average number of backlinks for page one SERP results on Google is 756,000. Holy cow! How can you get three quarters of a million backlinks?

Looking more closely, you can see that the top four results all belong to WebMD and the Mayo Clinic, and they each have over a million backlinks. Once you get beyond those articles, you find that the next website only has 650 backlinks. By the time you get to the bottom of the page, the last link only has 14 backlinks. Remember the story about the two guys being chased by a bear? "I don't have to be a fast runner, I just need to be faster than you!" Same thing here. Your initial backlink target is 15. If you've followed the other rules of SRO I've outlined in this section, you probably won't even need that. Many page one links are there because of one overriding factor, like the Mayo Clinic having a million backlinks. The SEO of the articles themselves is often horrible. You can get ahead of the competition by being a better "all around" competitor.

Create a checklist
Being good at everything is hard, unless you develop a checklist for all the pieces you need to create all of it, using the sections above as your guideline. Every business is different, so some parts of this section won't

work very well for some businesses, while they work exceptionally well for others. For example, if you don't have an online store, it's hard to create backlinks from your product listings, because you don't have any. But creating that checklist for everything you post is important, and sticking to it will be your key to long term success with business marketing online.

The Second Driver

Content Marketing

I used to call this section "Site Design", but I realized that this implied the concept that the site was designed once and then finished. In actuality, nothing could be further from the truth. Your actual "site design" is probably the fastest and easiest part of creating a website. You pick a look, a color scheme, add your logo, and you're done. That's site design. It's the quickest, easiest, and cheapest part of building websites. In the last ten years, the entire concept of "Content Marketing" has caught on, and the world has caught up with us.

Content Marketing is the real work of creating your online marketing platform. This is where you engage the search engines, engage your audience, and generally present the ongoing story of your business.

IMPORTANT: *I am going to make a point right now of saying that because technology changes so rapidly, there's almost no reason whatsoever to write out extensive details on which templates, themes or plugins to use with your Online Marketing Platform. We spend dozens of hours a week just staying up to date on the plugins and themes we use for our clients, and many more hours staying abreast of the latest changes in other marketing platforms. So, which is better? Wordpress? Infusionsoft? HubSpot? Squarespace? Marketo? The answer is far more dependent on who is asking and when you ask than you can really imagine. And now, with the introduction of AI to help with both site building and content creation, we have had another seismic shift in the technology marketplace. In response, we have monthly calls for our clients so they can just get the quick updates they need.*

Having said that, there are some trends and underlying themes that remain the same, regardless of the technology or web based platform. If you choose a platform other than WordPress (and unless you have a couple metric tons of money to develop your own platform that is just LIKE WordPress, I have no idea why you'd make that choice), you'll have to translate the basic concepts into the plugins or extensions available to your software.

Many people think a website is designed first, but that really is putting the cart before the horse. You need to know how your content will interact with search engines way before you start to imagine what you site will look like. A pretty site may appeal to your friends and family, but it won't do anything to help you be found by new customers. In fact, many of the slickest, prettiest sites on the internet are nearly impossible to find, because the fancy images, slideshows and embedded flash video mean absolutely nothing to the Google algorithm[4].

The most important things on your website are the words and how they are written. Notice there are two parts to this sentence. Like the images, if you don't present the words properly, you will not only give up any SRO advantage you might get from your content, but if you do it incorrectly, you can actually harm your site's SERP rankings. It's an important distinction to understand, but fortunately the line between "does nothing" and "hurts my site" is pretty broad, and as you'll understand soon, pretty easy to avoid.

And the really good news is that there's one way to do all of this, do it well, and do it fast.

Wordpress

Wordpress is the underlying website software for over 50% of the sites you see on the internet. Before you dismiss it as "just for blogs", (which is what I did for over two years, by the way), you need to understand the simple fact that Google, and all the other search engines, are designed to read WordPress sites. Yes, WordPress is

---

[4] There is a way to make your images help with your SRO, but it is a technical function, not an aesthetic one

so big and so dominant in the market that Google, Yahoo, Bing, and all the others are especially designed to respond to the things that can be built naturally into a WordPress site. Now, this is not a commercial for WordPress, but I have to say that I tried building parallel sites for small businesses, and it simply wasn't as effective as what business owners were able to do with the WordPress sites I built for them. There's no point in reinventing the wheel. Whatever your business is, there's no reason to have anything but a WordPress site as the foundation. Certainly, you may need to have extra pages with very narrow features and purposes, but those can be added on and "around" your WordPress gravity well. If that doesn't convince you, then perhaps the fact that the biggest names in internet marketing, such as Jeff Walker (who has been responsible for over half a BILLION dollars in internet sales) has a WordPress site for this main page. If you aren't thinking that's good enough, then perhaps the fact that BestBuy.com is a WordPress site will settle it for you. Obviously, these people can afford anything they want for websites, but they choose the exact same platform that you can have, as a small business owner... for free.

What's not to love?

So although everything I'm about to discuss in terms of content design will be in the context of a WordPress platform, it can be applied to DIY sites, Joomla sites, DreamWeaver sites, Squarespace, Wix, etc, etc. Work with your developer to make the upgrades to those other platforms, or if you don't have a developer, then consider experimenting with a parallel WordPress site until you are ready to migrate your old site to your new online marketing platform. It's not that hard, especially if you have GoDaddy as your hosting company, because they let you take your experimental site and "move" it directly over to your regular site location with a single keystroke. One minute, they're on your old site. The next, they're seeing your beautiful new online marketing platform, completely built with all the bells and whistles your old site needed but you couldn't get included.

Let's talk about the five basic elements that all good marketing platforms (we use this phrase instead of the old "website" name, because it is far more accurate). These five elements should be included on every Online Marketing Platform small business owners build, for they address the five basic ways customers want to interact with businesses on the web.

Homepage

Every Online Marketing Platform (OMP)[5] has to have a home page, or primary landing page. Wherever else people might eventually land, this is the page that many people will see first, regardless of what they find in the search engines or on social media. Given that fact, this page must have an easy to use navigation bar, good information and images describing your product or service, multimedia, and it should be MOBILE FRIENDLY. That does NOT mean that they can zoom in on it with a pinch of their fingers. It means the OMP itself is responsive and adjusts to the screen size and resolution automatically. Over 50% of all "hits" on local business websites are now happening on mobile devices. If you haven't done this properly, either through responsive cascading style sheets, or via simple mobile redirect to an augmented home page, then you are actually hurting yourself tremendously.

Contact Us

Your second requirement for your OMP is a "Contact Us" page. This page needs to contain the following information:

1. Your business name and hours of operation

---

[5] You really won't find the phrase "Online Marketing Platform" the way I use it online, except in my material. For now, we are the only ones using this new phraseology, but we think it is really important to be accurate and up to date in our efforts, regardless of what the rest of the business owners are doing. I hope you feel the same way.

2. Street address, if you have one

3. PHONE NUMBER (and there's special info on that which I will explain in a bit)

4. A link to either Google Maps or the ability to copy/paste the address into iMaps

5. An email link with your email address spelled out clearly

6. A form for people to contact you.

As I said above, the phone number needed special handling. There are two schools of thought on this, and they can both apply to a single business, but it is up to you to know which rule to apply, and when. If you have a toll free number that you want to use, then I specifically encourage you NOT to put it in HTML text if you are paying for that service by the minute. Why? Because there are evil people out there who send little spambots out to scrub websites all day and all night long, gathering phone numbers so telemarketers can call on you. You probably don't want to pay for that, so the trick is to make your 800 number an IMAGE, rather than the actual text. The spambots can't recognize a PICTURE of your phone number.

However, if you are a local business, you want your prospective customers to be able to contact you as easily as possible. This is one of those areas where I told you we would be coordinating different pieces of the marketing program to get them to work together. In this case, if you put the phone number in as text, using the regular format XXX-XXX-XXXX, then people with smartphones will be able to dial you simply by clicking on the number. There's no special coding involved. A good smartphone knows a phone number when it sees one. You can leverage that little bit of technology to make your business look that much more sophisticated. And since over half your customers are going to be finding you on their mobile phones, this is absolutely crucial to your site design.

About Us

The third thing your site has to have is an About Page. The about page is where you tell your story. The internet has replaced the town square, or local Chamber of Commerce, in many ways. People go here to find out what it is that makes your business unique. What makes you special. Customers want to know more than your company tagline. Taglines are a dime a dozen. They want, mostly, to know about the PEOPLE who make up your business. If they dial the phone, what kind of people will be on the other end of the line? The About page is where you give your story. You can explain why you are the RIGHT choice for certain people looking for specific solutions. The About page is where you really lay it on the line, explaining just what makes you the first, best choice in town. It's not about bragging. It's about facts. If you have 26 years of experience repairing commercial refrigeration units and have a track record for getting people's units back working within 90 minutes 90% of the time, then by God this is the place to say that! You know what your customers' hot buttons are, and this is where you can hit them right between the eyes with it.

Our Products/Services

The fourth page every website needs is a Products or Services Page. Your Products/Services page is where you get into details about the kinds or types of products or services you provide. If you are a manufacturer, this is where you get to list the full line of items you make. If you are a reseller or retailer, this is your online store. You need a solid list of products here, and brand names, listed properly on this page. This page alone can account for a LOT of your searches in Google or Yahoo!. But we'll come back to that later, when we start to integrate SRO into your website.

If you provide a service, then this is the page where you describe it in detail. Get into the nitty gritty, and use all those long tail key words you found in your SRO research. Use those key phrases as headings, in fact, and you will help Google find you that much easier. (A heading is denoted by the use of an h1, h2 or h3 style code for the text. By making your keywords into headings for paragraphs, you are alerting the search engines that this is a very important subject on your OMP.

The WordPress dropdown selection box looks something like this:

Just making the text bold and large will not alert the search engines. You must use an h-tag to get the full effect you desire. Here's a trick, though. You should only use Heading 2 (h2) or Heading 3 (h3), as Google doesn't pay attention to anything under h3. In fact, there is even dispute now as to whether h3 even shows up in the algorithm any more. In addition, too many people attempted to flood the system by putting everything in h1, so Google has recently taken to ignoring h1 content. H2 is your best bet for the important stuff, but make sure there is an h1 headline above it. Google notices when things don't flow through a natural taxonomy, and it downgrades the results if they aren't in proper order. Don't have an h-2 without an h-1, and don't have an h-3 without an h-2.

Now, the Fifth Element you must put in your website is one thing everybody seems to question, and I don't know why. The reasons for it are way beyond question, and the reasons against it... well, there's usually only ONE reason people cite against it...is just an excuse. In fact, this fifth element of your website design is so important, I would suggest that if you had to ONLY do one of these pieces, then THIS is the piece you should do. Now, remember, I'm not talking about the Five Drivers here, but the five elements of Site Design, which is just ONE of the Five Drivers.

What's this element? I think a few of you already have it. That's right. It's your blog. The blog is the single most important element you can have on your website, and as I said before, if you only had to have ONE element, it would be the blog.

Why's that? It's easy. Google HATES old websites. What's an old website? You've seen them. Flashing text, black backgrounds with yellow text. Lots of text. I mean LOTS and LOTS and LOTS of text on the home page. And pretty much nothing has been changed on that homepage in the last 30 days. No, I don't mean 30 months. I mean 30 days. Your content HAS to be fresh and dynamic. It has to show Google that your site is still alive, updated and worth visiting.

There are millions of what I call "zombie sites" out there on the internet. Not just millions, but TENS of millions... even billions of sites. They're dead. They're still accessible, but they're dead. They're zombies. They are the undead of the internet. When I'm your customer and I see you have a zombie site, I assume your business is as undead as your website, and move on to the next one, hoping for somebody with a pulse.

The Blog

The blog lets you keep your website active, alive, vibrant and current. It tells people that yes, you are indeed still in business. I cannot emphasize enough the importance of having your homepage be an active collection of recent material. So if you aren't blogging, if you aren't telling your customers, and Google, that you're still in business and actively accepting new customers, then you might as well not even bother with going into business today.

I know that sounds strong, but how many of you think that you could run your business successfully if you only had half of your customer base? Don't give up half the business. This system really does allow you to leverage up your time and energy so that you can make the most of your working day.

We first implemented this strategy by adding a Facebook activity block to the home page. This worked very well for our small businesses, and you'll see that many of our clients still do it. Some people are just better at keeping their social media updated, and so we used to give them a way to do it.

This, however, isn't the best long term strategy for your business, and for two very important reasons.

Why you can't count on Facebook or X (Twitter) to demonstrate your liveliness

Social media websites are just an adjunct to your actual OMP. When you post material on their sites, that is exactly where it stays. It may provide a LINK back to your site, but in the end, the content you create "over there" STAYS "over there". It does nothing for your own organic SRO. This may not seem like an important distinction, but we have to understand that just because we SEE a difference on your home page because you posted a status update on Facebook doesn't mean Google sees the difference. Google only sees the HTML code that drags in the information from Facebook (or X), but doesn't recognize the changing nature of what this code drags over. As far as Google is concerned, you've not changed or added anything on your page. Although your potential customers can see you've posted something new and fresh, the search engines are absolutely blind to it.

Own your platform

The second reason you want to blog instead of using social media is even more important, although more philosophical in nature. You want to "own" your platform. You want to have full access and control over your content, how it is displayed, and how it is searched. By creating your content on a social media platform, you are really (and legally) granting them full control over your content. Social media platforms come and go (Remember MySpace? Me neither…) and we don't know what will be the popular platform with your market in a couple years. By owning your content creation space, you can simply use the new social media platforms to direct traffic to the same place you've been sending them for years. And all the content you've created for years stays put, increasing the depth of your gravity well over time. Which brings me to another important point…

There is no such thing as a website launch for an OMP

An Online Marketing Platform never actually "launches". There is no date on which you site is "complete" and you can then forget about it and move onto other marketing projects. An Online Marketing Platform is never, ever finished. It is always a work in progress.

Certainly, you may have a "Go Live" date, in which the public can begin accessing your new site, but this is not the single event it used to be in the days when we put brochures online for customers and called them "websites". In fact, this is perhaps the single greatest difference between a website and an OMP. A website is a presentation, whereas an OMP is a conversation. You don't have a conversation with someone by walking into the room, reading a paragraph or two, then walking out. That would actually just be a bit weird.

However, that is exactly what traditional websites do. They wait for people to show up, shove information at them, and then wait for the people to leave. In today's world, you have to engage your visitors, finding out what they want, and then deliver it to them in bite sized morsels. The website interaction is more like dating, where you slowly get to know each other, and then after a respectable amount of time, decide whether or not you're going to get into the relationship.

A blog lets you do that. People can see your material, reply to it either on your site, or perhaps on social media, and you can answer their questions, or reply to their comments. It's the next best thing to having someone walk into your showroom. In fact, it may be better, because evicting troublemakers doesn't involve calling the police: you use the "Trash" button and the offensive reply just disappears. You've got the power.

A website is a static event. You pay someone to create it, like a written report, and then it is published and you are done with the project. An Online Marketing Platform is a constant effort, and this is a GREAT thing. The ability to constantly and consistently adjust and adapt your message is what real marketing is all about. We used to have to pay tens of thousands of dollars to bring in focus groups over and over and over again until we had a marketing message that "worked". Now, we can experiment and adjust to the changes in the marketplace every day. Let's explain the difference by using a real world example: the introduction of the Affordable Care Act.

Whether you approved of the law or not, this legislation had a massive impact on insurance agents nationwide. The difference between a successful agency and a failure can be understood by how they were able to respond to the rapid change in their marketplace.

A traditional agency, with a normal website, needed to wait until they had a full grasp on Obamacare, all of the legislation's nuances and loopholes, and only then could they launch a new website with definitive information on what their clients should do under the new law. As it stood, this process took almost a year.

Contrast that with an agency that had a dynamic Online Marketing Platform. The OMP agency started on day one, grabbing articles from the web and "interpreting" the meaning of the latest rules, based upon the best undestanding at the moment. Clients from their agency had immediate access to a professional opinion on the important elements of the law. As the law changed, or as the media discussed different aspects, the OMP agency was able to respond within minutes, if they felt it was important, to the latest revelations. Their client base could be assured that this insurance agency was staying right on top of the issue.

But it's not only the OMP agency's clients that would know this. The agency with the static website also had clients that had the same questions. When doing Google searches for answers, the OMP agency would show up because they had some of the newest, most pertinent answers to their questions. The static website agency had their usual customer service phone number on their homepage, and they just hoped people might call if they had questions. As more people went to the OMP site for answers, you can be assured that when it came time to sign up, they were, by and large, going to work with the agency that had been an authority in the field, rather than an agency which only appeared to be adding Affordable

Care Act information when they could no longer avoid talking about it.

But what if you publish information that is wrong?

This is MUCH less of a problem than you think, and in fact is just another opportunity for success. If you have an article that contains bad information, you don't actually delete the article! Instead, you add a note to the TOP of the article, saying that the information has now been updated and they can find more information on the subject in the NEW article you wrote, and then you provide a link to the new article. Don't give up the SRO of the old article, nor sacrifice the opportunity for an internal link to a related topic. Changing your mind in your blog isn't a problem; it's a gold mine.

This is just one way in which a blog can be used to attract and retain new customers. Don't expect every blog article you post to grab thousands of readers right away. The fact is, the more articles you write for your blog, the deeper and deeper your gravity well becomes. It's not just Google that will measure your gravity well, either. If I'm a prospective customer and I see you have written two articles on a subject, I might consider you knowledgeable on the topic, depending upon the content. However, if I land on your page and I see you have authored sixty-five articles over the span of five years, I'm going to see that you are not only quite aware of many facets of the topic, but that you have been in the business for years, and are a reputable, reliable source of consistent service for your clients. You've sold me with your thoroughness and your consistency.

What I'm really saying here is that your Online Marketing Platform should never, ever be finished. We no longer call it "site design", but rather "content design". We are far more interested in taxonomy instead of aesthetics, as this is a reflection of how your prospective customers might find your information. Therefore, let's talk a little bit about taxonomy.

Taxonomy: How people find stuff on your OMP

Growing up, you probably only ever heard the word "taxonomy" used in biology class, where we were learning how to catgegorize plants or animals. You know, tarantulas were under the category "Arachnid". Restaurant menus have great categories. Sandwiches and salads might be under "Lunches", while fried green tomatoes and hummus and chips could be under "Appetizers". The human brain, in fact, automatically creates taxonomies. It's how we categorize the (literally) millions of things we see in our lifetimes. We don't provide any more detail to a taxonic category than our needs require. There may be 17 different models of a Hyundai Sonata for 2025, but unless you own one, you probably just categorize ALL Hyundais under the heading "Hyundai".

The point is, how you categorize the information in your OMP should be directly focused on how your customers would think to look for it.

Let's look at the two basic ways a Wordpress OMP runs its taxonomy: Categories and Tags.

Categories

Categories function exacly as you would expect them to work. If I have a website about birds, I might have categories of Land Birds or Water Fowl. Or I might decide to have "Exotic Birds" and "Wild Birds". These distinctions are important because your business needs to deliver the categories in the way your customers would search for it. If I'm running a farm-focused website, I might have categories of Chickens and Ducks, or Layers and Broilers. You know what your categories are for your business, and it is absolutely crucial that all your posts, pages and products are categorized appropriately for your customers.

Making sure your categories are right has two huge benefits:

1. Good categories make it easy for prospective customers to find exactly what they want on your OMP

2. Well constructed categories make it easy for Google to understand what's available on your site, and give weight to the things that have the most entries under a specific category.

By creating your categories properly for your customers, you are engaging in exactly the kind of efforts that search engines reward heavily with high rankings. It's a win/win.

Tags

Tags are words or phrases that serve as a secondary way of organizing the information on your site. These are things that may not be "big" enough to have their own categories, but will really help prospective customers find specific things that interest them.

Sticking with the restaurant example, you may have several items on the menu that are vegetarian friendly. Instead of creating a whole category for a few vegetarian options, you can use a "Vegetarian" tag. Then, when someone clicks on that word in your tag listing, all the dishes that you have tagged as "Vegetarian" will come up. You may not want to overtly advertise that your firehouse chili is actually made with soy crumbles, but a vegetarian will be ecstatic to find it in a tag search.

Keep the number of tags you use across your site to a minimum, though. Not every detail deserves a tag, and your important tags shouldn't be lost in a deluge of "Gluten Free", "Made with some organic ingredients", "Contains dairy", "No preservatives", "Cooked to order", and "Fresh made daily".

Let's go in to a little more detail on how we use categories for an Online Marketing Platform. In working with a restaurant, we decided that the previous website had used a taxonomy that didn't really fit how people hunted for food. It had reflected the way the restaurant owners ran the business, rather than how the patrons ordered the food. So, rather than having the OMP categorized by "Food", "Drinks", "Catering" and "Entertainment", we created master headings for

"Lunch", "Dinner" and "Drinks", then provided sub categories for each heading, with things like "Sandwiches", "Pasta", "Seafood" or "Desserts".

Fortunately, a Wordpress-based OMP allows you to easily create these results pages for the headings, and a single item can appear in multiple places without having to be entered multiple times. By using a category of "Sandwiches", and making sure the "Sandwich" heading had "Lunches" as a parent category, we could easily create the necessary results pages within the OMP. You click on the header "Sandwiches" on the home page, and you will be sent to a page that lists all the sandwiches available.

Images: the secret weapon for SRO

Here's a quick tip for getting your site onto a page one SERP a little faster. This particular trick has worked wonders for some of my clients, because they are dealing in retail products in which they are competing with a lot of different retailers to get you to buy the same product. Frankly, this is about the lowest of low hanging fruit you can grab if you happen to be in this situation, but it can also help you in B2B and professional services if you play it right.

A picture's worth a thousand words, but if you can't find that picture, it's worthless. Photos can really liven up your OMP, and a featured image is a mandatory element of any post or article you create, but the fact is, your photos don't have to just take up storage in your database. Pictures have attributes, and because search engines can't "see" what your picture is, you have to tell it. This is an opportunity you shouldn't waste. Perhaps the best way to explain this is to show you an example. Let's go back to our saddle store so you can really understand what I'm saying.

You have a Wintec saddle for sale. It's about a $500 item. People looking for Wintecs can be very particular about their saddle. However, they are generally very loose in their searches for their saddle. They may only put in the name and model they are looking for. In this case, let's say it's the Wintec 500. This is where the fun begins.

You see, the manufacturer has a large website with about a thousand images of all different saddles of all different models, styles and colors. Because of this, they have a coded name for all their images, usually based on a SKU number, or perhaps an in-house abbreviation of some kind. In the case of a black Wintec 500 dressage saddle, the manufacturer for this one saddle has the images named as follows:

W_500_Dressage_blk1.jpg, W_500_Dressage_blk2.jpg, W_500_Dressage_blk3.jpg, etc.

To the manufacturer, this code makes perfect sense, and they can easily identify the subject of the image quickly, and will allow them to sort the images easily in folders. But because of this system they have, they cause a cascade failure across the internet that you can use to your advantage. Here's what happens next.

Most small businesses are either frugal, or just plain lazy when it comes to adding images to their websites. If they know Verhan has high quality studio shots of their saddles on the corporate website, they will most often just go out to the website and "steal" the pictures by downloading them to their own hard drive, then uploading them to their websites. In doing so, they usually replicate the photo exactly as it was on the corporate site. Therefore, they, too, are populating the web with photos that have the same names: W_500_Dressage_blk1.jpg.

Can you imagine any person in the world searching for a saddle by looking up "W_500_Dressage_blk1.jpg"? It's because they don't. They will search for "wintec 500 saddle". So that's where you win. Even if you are "stealing" the photo from the corporate site (and I don't advocate you doing this unless it is part of your reseller agreement that you can use their imagery for your own marketing purposes) all you have to do is RENAME the photo before you upload it to your OMP. That's it.

When Google returns its search results, it will often have a row of images that also match the search terms, right on page one. If every other reseller in the world is using some cryptic internal code, and you are the only one with the real name of the product attached to the image, then you will be the first image people see on the SERP.

The name of the image isn't the only place where you can score a hit. You also have alt-tags and titles for the image. You can fill these out as completely as you did the name of the photo, and it will reinforce the accuracy of the search with the engines. If you are using a WordPress OMP, then when you upload the image, you can change the URL to which the image links (and is hardwired to do so) in the image attributes section. If you change the URL to the page where you are selling that particular item, rather than just the link to the image, then when people click on the image on Google it will take them directly to your item's sale page on your website.

And then, when Google notices that your web page is getting more traffic, and fewer bounces than other sites because you have provided the prospective customers with a lot of useful information on the topic, and perhaps other items they might consider, Google will reward you by moving your sales page further and further up towards the top of the search results.

I've actually seen where a website got more useful traffic off its images than it did off its Pay Per Click links, and it cost them nothing but a few extra minutes per day to adjust their images appropriately.

SRO in Content Design

There are a few other things you should keep in mind while continuing to create your content for your site. We're going to look at three things you can do to improve your searchability, while at the same time improving the READability of your posts.

The first one we've already discussed, and that was the use of h-tags when formatting your text. If you have a sub-header in an article, and it is FIRST an important element of THIS particular article, AND it is a term that prospective customers might be searching, then use the h-tag to create that header in your article. You may not want it to be as big and gaudy as the h1 tag, so use the h2 or h3. Any of those three pieces of HTML code will tell the search engines that this is an important part of your article and it should pay attention to it. *The key is to make these headings match the long-tailed keywords you selected for your site.*

The second thing you should keep in mind is the list. This serves two purposes, so don't miss any opportunities to utilize it in your OMP efforts. When you are writing an article, people love to see bulleted lists of the key features/steps/instructions you are giving. Whether you use bullets or numbers should be based on the nature of the content. Don't title an article, "Five Things You Can Say to Get Hired", then use bullets for the five things. Use numbers. But, if you are saying, "Here are some key points to remember when interviewing:", use bullets. Don't imply an order where none exists.

Lists have been shown to increase the readership of an online article by as much as 200%, but they also serve as "flags" for the search engines. They pay particularly close attention to the content of your list, since you have made it a point to highlight the material. Using the "list" style function in the OMP dashboard is a fast and effective way of improving your SRO.

Perhaps the most important thing you can do, however, is to reference yourself within your website. I don't mean talk about your personal life, but rather to talk about the features that can be found elsewhere on your site. So, if you happen to be a personal injury attorney specializing in asbestos related cases, then when you are writing an article about recent awards for claims, you might include a sentence like, "the awards were received when the plaintiffs worked closely with their asbestos injury attorneys to document all their expenses…". The underlined text is a link to your "About me", or "Services" page, where people can contact you to see if you are a good candidate to represent them.

This "internal linking" is perhaps the single most frequent mistake business owners make when creating content. People forget to provide references to THEMSELVES when writing their articles, thinking that just because the customer has come to the page they will take the time and effort to poke around and find the necessary information. Forget it. They won't. You have to spoon feed it to them, carefully and calmly, without appearing pushy or aggressive. You're simply making it easy for them to buy from you. And, naturally, these internal links also count towards your SRO, by as much as 50% according to some new research. If you maintain an internally cohesive platform, then Google is going to take you much more seriously. All the connections you make within your articles just increase your "gravity well" by tying those pieces together.

Make a list, check it twice

We must never forget that the primary purpose of your Online Marketing Platform is to create a unique space where you can communicate directly with your prospective customers, sharing with them information and products that they find interesting. Your job is to hold on to them and bring them back to your site as many times as you can, even after they have bought from you. In fact, the first purchase may only be the beginning of a very long, profitable relationship. But the fact is, most people will not buy from you the first time they land on your site. Or the second time, or the third. They are investigating you. When you see a conversion rate of 3%, that means 97% of the people who visited your site didn't buy anything. Don't worry about them. They just aren't ready yet.

But to get them to BE ready to buy from you, it is imperative that you have a way to stay in contact with them. The easiest, most effective way to do this is to ask them for their email address. That way, when you have something new or exciting to tell them, you can just drop them a line and let them know. You are being a good information source, and they are learning to trust you.

Unfortunately, that's where most small businesses STOP their most profitable form of marketing, and get little to no results from it.

Keep that point in mind, because we are going to expand upon it after we discuss the next of the Five Drivers of Business Marketing Online.

The Third Driver

Social Media

Social Media has been the mutated offspring of the internet, capitalizing on the inherent human desire to be a part of a group. When we understand what role social media plays in people's lives, we will be better able to work with it to achieve our goal of growing our businesses. We will also be able to avoid the pitfalls that many small businesses (and large ones!) fall into while attempting to advertise in this new media.

Let's start with the basic understanding that humans are herd animals. Not all humans, but most of them, seek to find connectedness in their lives and daily activities. We want to know that we belong, and that people care about us. As we became a more transient society, with a high percentage of people moving away from their home towns and its close-knit social groups, we found it easier to move to new places... *and just stay indoors*. We have learned to avoid meeting our neighbors, for fear of not liking them (or more likely, of not being liked!), and we watched a lot of television. In the 1990s, this became an epidemic, where "gated communities" contained lots of people who had never even met each other. I knew several families who had lived in such communities for five years or more, and still could not actually name the people that lived on either side of them.

It was into this environment that social media was born. The youth are the first to find solutions to problems that adults didn't quite know they had, and that was the case here. With forums and groups, people were able to connect and discuss specific topics. In 1997, AOL introduced us to "Instant Messaging", and suddenly we were having real time communication with people we knew. In 2002, "Friendster" was launched to create a network of people you really knew in real life. It added 3 million members in its first three months (almost 1% of the internet users at the time!) Friendster was cloned, with the code written in less than two weeks, and the new product was introduced:

MySpace.com

This is where it became confusing. Many other sites, including popular networking sites like LinkedIn, or video sharing sites like YouTube, began to see the future of social media, and they began to adapt their platforms to allow people to "follow" each other, add themselves to circles of friends, or simply watch certain groups/ discussions whenever they chose. But none of them pulled it together in the right way until 2004. That is when the virtual world had a seismic shift.

Facebook is born

Love it or hate it, Facebook (now Meta) was the fusion of all the existing social media platforms, and with the addition of a few more features, something finally "clicked" with the public. Although originally planned as a way of connecting college students (it was started at Harvard, and in the first month over half of the student body had signed up!), Facebook became a way for people to connect, follow, watch and communicate across the country. We could stay in touch with our old friends, and meet new ones through them. This was hugely important at satisfying our "need to belong". We could easily find like-minded individuals, and reinforce our sense of self-worth and value to society. Nothing else can explain the vast and rapid growth of Facebook, which went from 5.5 million users in December of 2005, to 100 million users in August of 2008, and cracked the one BILLION user mark just eight years after launching. People don't engage unless they have a strong emotion giving them the energy to do so, and Facebook created that emotional energy surge at just the right time in our societal evolution. It really was that heavy, and it really was that significant, and keeping that in mind, let me show you one of the evolutionary paths that failed miserably.

As all these people started getting together, people realized that all these eyeballs were worth something. In fact, they were worth a lot. But they had to be approached properly, or it simply wasn't going to work. To explain this distinction, let me give you an example of a social media discussion. You'll see where the train comes off the tracks.

> TOM: Man, I had such an amazing weekend. We went to the movies, then we just walked on the beach until sunrise. It was amazing!

> SUSAN: Did you know that Sherry was pregnant? I'm so excited for her!

> NATE: We really rocked the house last night. The audience was INCREDIBLE! Super shoutout thanks to everybody in Houston for such a great reception!

TERRY: Seven billion people on this planet, and I don't have any friends. Why doesn't anybody like me?

ABC-AUTO-SALES: Great cars cheap! Call today and ask for Chip. 813-555-1212

LUKE: Hey guys. We're throwing a party for Lisa's retirement. Anybody got ideas about where to go and what to get her?

Did you see the "sore thumb" post? It's pretty obvious. The guy from the auto dealership is using social media as an advertising medium. He doesn't care about the community. He doesn't belong to any group. He's just standing out there, waving his banner, hoping somebody notices. Except that doesn't work well in social media, because the emphasis isn't ON media. It's on SOCIAL.

Here's the trick, though. Did you notice the OTHER "commercial entity" that was also posting in that thread of comments? Did you see the business that was reaching out to its customers, acknowledging their participation in a corporate event?

It was NATE, who obviously plays in a band that performed in Houston the previous night. He used social media to interact with the band's fans, reaching out to them to acknowledge their efforts and what made them special to the band. The message was personal, and it was sincere.

Given this emotional context for social media, it becomes obvious why emotions must be a serious part of what you say or do when using social media to communicate with your customers and prospects. This is probably as good a place as any to discuss the importance of emotion in the marketing of a product.

There's a sign on the wall of my studio that says "What people don't feel, people don't remember". It may sound like a bumper sticker, but in fact, it is well documented (although sometime debated) in psychological research. In 1977, Brown and Kulik posited that there was a biological mechanism in the brain that leads to remembering important, but unexpected events with near photographic accuracy. Although the accuracy of the recounted memory may be subject to degradation, the details of the memory seem to be retained better when the memory is repeatedly recounted. In fact, my own research into neuroplasticity suggests that an emotional event touches on many more areas of the brain, and thus creates a stronger neural "impact" zone. The more synapses that are created by a new memory, the more likely that memory is to "embed" itself into your regular thought processes. When you repeat the details to yourself, you are reinforcing and strengthening that new set of synapse connections. Generally, you repeat the details (usually verbally while recounting the event to others) and they become more and more deeply entrenched as the synapse connections become stronger and stronger.

Now, let's put that into English.

For this example, we are going to think of the human brain as a bunch of very thin, soft wires, all laid out in neat rows, very close to each other, but not touching. Each of these wires has energy flowing through it, but because none of them are touching, the energy just passes through them from one end to the other. But then, something happens. Imagine an incident that occurs is like a small rubber ball that drops onto the wires. When the ball impacts the wires, it causes them to bend and warp, and some will touch each other. If the impact of the ball is strong enough, these new connections between the wires may "stick". As these new connections are made, the way the energy flows through them is altered and those new pathways for the energy change the energy.

I know this is getting a bit esoteric, but stay with me. There's a reason for it.

Now, two things will cause the new connections to stick, and stick hard. Once those connections stick, they become permanent memories. What are the two things?

One is the weight of the rubber ball. If it is a BIG event, even if it doesn't have a lot of emotional importance to you, it will stick. Maybe your office moved to a big, new building. It didn't matter to you or your work or your marriage, but the move itself was big, and now that you are in the new building, it is a constant reminder that it is not the old building.

The second thing that can cause the new connections to stick is the energy that is being pushed through the wires. If you have a highly emotional event going on, then your brain is creating and channeling massive amounts of excess energy through its wiring. Whether it's fear, or sympathy, or sexual arousal, this energy is being channeled through the wires of your neural network. And if you have an event that makes an impact while this increased energy is flowing, it can cause the wires to "fuse" together from the excess heat of the transfer (metaphorically speaking, of course). Once the energy makes the jump, just like real electric wires, they don't want to let go. As long as you still have the emotional energy tied to the event, the new connections between the wires will become stronger and stronger. And, the more you repeat the details of the event by recounting it to others, the more you will arouse the initial energy, and thus you will cement the connections in place.

Now that is an amateurish mash-up of a lot of brain biochemistry, shoved into one paragraph so that you can have a usable context for understanding marketing. It almost seems mercenary to discuss it in this fashion, but I'm not here to put a value judgment on it. I'm just here to tell you how it works, and why it works. But the fact remains, regardless of the morality, it does work.

This also explains why some people will get some facts exactly right when they recount an event, and others can be completely fictitious, but still be thought of as entirely real and accurate. As we recount the story, we will describe details we absolutely remember, and as we engage in the description, we will sometimes embellish the real memories with ones we think SHOULD be there, because they make sense. For example, we will remember that when we heard about Dad being in a car accident, we were standing with Mom, who was wearing her blue coat with the teal scarf. We remember it that way because Mom always wore that scarf with that coat, however it turns out that the scarf was an accessory that was added two months AFTER the car accident. But, because we identify that coat with that scarf, we overlay the two memories and they, although inaccurate, become one. And we will be absolutely certain it is 100% true, to the point where the receipt for the blue scarf being dated two months after the accident must be some kind of mistake, and it will be dismissed as some kind of inexplicable anomaly. The human mind is that confident.

I know, because I've done it. The year was 1977. It had to be, because I was old enough to be hanging out at Dave's house playing wiffleball, but it was before we moved away from Charlestown in 1978. I remember Dave telling us about a movie he had seen that was simply outrageously funny. It was a spoof of disaster movies called, "Airplane". He told us about the jokes, and about how it was so different from any other movie they had made.

Sounds like a perfectly legitimate memory, doesn't it?

Except "Airplane" wasn't released until 1980.

Somewhere in my mind the incident of someone describing that movie has become overlaid on top of the memory of playing wiffleball at Dave's house. They are inextricably intertwined, yet they must be separate.

So what does any of this have to do with online marketing? In a word: everything.

If we are going to be seeking to influence the way people think, it's good that we understand the process by which they think, learn, and pay attention. It takes a knowledge of the system if you expect to use it to your advantage.

The first thing we have to look at is emotional sincerity. It is the easiest, fastest, most direct way to get somebody to notice (and remember!) you or your business. It's also the easiest thing for a prospective customer to sniff out as phony. Content that is forced, aggressive or out of character is quickly recognized as mercenary and will cost you dearly.

Web 2.0

Web 2.0 was the phrase coined about fifteen years ago to describe the seismic shift in how people related to the internet. Some people wrongly suggest that "Web 2.0" simply means "social media". That's like confusing an MP3 player with the music it contains in its memory. The music is the reason the MP3 player was invented, and in the same way, Web 2.0 was the reason social media came into prevalence.

So, what is this fundamental shift known as "Web 2.0"? Perhaps the best way to understand it is by looking at Web 1.0, and then drawing the contrast.

In the earliest iterations of the internet, the idea was for people to be able to go to a source, like a library, and find the information they wanted. Remember, the first web page was built by a research facility to help researchers find their information more easily. The result was predicated upon the user instigating the action by searching for a specific result. This information/action flow gave rise to one of the great internet powerhouses,

Google. Google specializes in delivering the information you want to see, based upon your inputting the key words that represent your desire. The flow is instigated by the user.

Web 2.0 reverses that process. In the new version, the information now finds the user, regardless of the user's input. When a user goes online, his identity is recognized and his interaction with the data is customized to match his interests and desires, based upon his previous online history. If you've spent any time on Facebook, then you've already seen this happening. Using a technology called "retargeting", eBay remembers what you last looked at on their site, and when you go over to Facebook, an ad for that item will appear on your Facebook newsfeed. What you like now follows you around the web. You can think of it as a bit creepy, like you're being stalked, but really it is just the wonders of technology that are allowing the web to customize your user experience to make it uniquely appropriate for you.

Really, there are only two ways this can happen. The user searches for the information, or the information searches for the user. I think that's why talk of Web 3.0 isn't terribly useful. The only things I've seen on this subject are just differences in website design, style, or coding languages. In fact, if I were to make a prediction about Web 3.0, it would be that the user is no longer required to even consciously interact with the web interface. In a leap into tomorrow, you would have the full library of the internet in your mind, and it would automatically overlay your real world experience. Your interface would give you descriptions and definitions of any and all objects it recognizes as something you probably don't know or understand. So, when you walk into a museum, you're not puzzled about whether a painting is by Monet or Renoir. Your interface automatically labels the paintings for you. Sound like science fiction? The fact is, Google Glass is already part way there. It won't take much more for a contact lens to accomplish all this, and more.

Some say that's just a further extension of Web 2.0, though, because it is still the information flow to you that makes the difference. I suggest it is 3.0 because the interface is gathering the information on your behalf and sending it to the internet in a streaming, live fashion BEFORE the web responds with advice and information.

So what does any of this have to do with business marketing online?

Again… everything.

By utilizing social media, and making it an integral part of your Online Marketing Platform, you are traveling to the place where your prospective customers are "hanging out", and you are engaging them in a way that no search engine could imagine. You are putting your business in front of them, but doing it in a way that is friendly, engaging and inviting. By using the social media driver properly, you are creating the kind of interaction that Web 2.0 is all about. You're moving your business into the 21st century.

In a nutshell, Web 1.0 was about being found by your actively searching customers. Web 2.0 is about you positively engaging with your customers, whether they are looking for you at that minute or not.

Action Steps

What we should do now is take all this theory and conceptual information and turn it into action steps that you can use to get the most out of your social media marketing efforts.

Step 1: Be sure your OMP has plenty of ways for people to share your content with their friends.

There are many plug ins available for free or for nominal fees that allow your readers or prospects to easily share your content via social media. Anybody who lands on one of your pages should be able to click one button and share your content via Facebook or email. Period. If nothing else, you must have those two options available.

Step 2: Be sure your website REMAINS the center of your customer experience.

I know way too many people who get hooked on posting content on social media directly. This is a huge mistake, because it puts your center of activity in somebody else's control. It is imperative that you create your content on your own platform, and then post a LINK to that content (with a summary or excerpt from it) on social media. By doing this, you are not only creating a unique user experience wherein you can have total influence over what your prospective customer sees, but you also have the ability to engage in that magical science called "retargeting" I discussed above. We'll talk more about that in a bit.

Step 3. Focus on Facebook. Forget about the rest (for now)

Yes, I said it, and yes, I mean it. You know the 80/20 rule? It's been abducted by Facebook and they are running away with it. The fact is, 81% of all shared content on the internet goes through one source and one source ONLY: Facebook. The corollary to that mathematical fact is that the other 19% of shared online content is divided between these (and other) social media channels:

- X
- LinkedIn
- Pinterest
- Reddit
- Tumblr
- Instagram
- TikTok
- Truth
- Pinterest
- Meetup
- WhatsApp
- Gettr
- YouTube

If you insist on using one of the other social media outlets, then make sure it receives your secondary attention. The only place where I would give even remotely equal attention to a second outlet is for Business-to-Business sales, and then I would just add LinkedIn. But I wouldn't spend much time monitoring it, and I certainly wouldn't create any specialized content for it.

Roughly 70% of Americans are on Facebook. By no coincidence, the other 30% are too old or too young to be on Facebook. Odds are about 80% or higher that whomever you wish to talk to is on Facebook, and you can find them there fairly easily. There are two ways to find them there, and they work together perfectly. Let's talk about target markets, and retargeting.

Unless you're living in the stone age (and honestly, I just found somebody last week who IS living in the stone age!) you have your personal Facebook Page, and then a separate Fan Page for your business. No, this is NOT a private Facebook account named after your business (that's what I saw last week). You will know whether you have your page set up right if you have to accept friend requests or not. If you have to give somebody permission to follow your page, you're doing it wrong.

You must have a Fan page that is dedicated to your one business. It needs to be focused and clean, using the same imagery as your OMP so that people are not confused. From within this fan page you will have the ability to do great things; the first of which is target marketing.

Target Marketing

Regardless of what media you attempt to use, the idea of target marketing is going to dominate your thinking. A target market is exactly that: a segment of the population that could be in the market for your product that you wish to target with your marketing message. In my book, target markets are broken into two broad categories. It is good to think about both, but in the end, Web2.0 will diminish the importance of them. You'll see why.

Demographics

Demographics is the classic concept of the target market. "I'm looking to talk to women aged 35-54 with household incomes over $75,000, two children and a professional career". You can choose those things, and they might deliver you a woman who would be interested in joining your Yoga studio. You will miss the woman who doesn't have kids, or the woman who is divorced and only making $65,000 a year. Your goal, however, is to hit the most LIKELY candidate for your product, and demographics let you do that. It is a way of focusing your marketing dollars in one area, instead of spreading the message so thin nobody actually notices.

Psychographics

This is where the fun begins. Let's imagine you're still doing the Yoga studio, but what you realize is that 94% of your clients all eat organic food. There is no intrinsic relationship between organic food and Yoga, but the psychological link there is, nonetheless. By using psychographics, you can now target women aged 35-54 who are interested in organic foods, and you may have a MUCH more focused audience for your Yoga studio marketing.

Combining them into one campaign

Facebook allows you to do both demographic and psychographic target marketing to your prospective customers. You can narrow down the field, not only to women aged 35-54, but even tighter if you wish. Let's talk about women who are approaching fifty years old. That's a pretty big benchmark. You can choose women who are 47 to 49 years of age, have an interest in Yoga, exercise or organic food, and live within a ten mile radius of your studio. You can then headline your ad with something like:

"Getting (uncomfortably) close to 50?"

And run a constant campaign whereby you are inviting these women to check out your "Reclaim your Youth" Yoga sessions on Tuesday and Thursday evenings. Depending upon your results, you can choose to spend as little as $1.00 a day. I have watched customers get tens of thousands of dollars of new business off campaigns that limited themselves to just $1 a day. That's because they narrowly targeted their ads to a very precise market, and then delivered to these people exactly what they would want to read.

That's the power of target marketing in Facebook. Honestly, I just made that whole Yoga thing up off the top of my head. You can do a MUCH better job with your business, regardless of the market you are in, the product you sell, or the way you have to deliver it. You know who comes in your door, and what subjects interest them. Use that knowledge to find more of these people.

But didn't I say social media wasn't about advertising? Doesn't that sound a whole lot like advertising?

Well, yes. But that's not the point. Sure, we can have ads running on Facebook, but that's not what you will be spending most of your time creating. Your job is to create content on your OMP, and then post a link to that content on Facebook.

Let's stay with the Yoga studio example. The owner may have an ad running on Mondays and Wednesdays, inviting people to her Tuesday and Thursday sessions, but during the other days of the week, she might be posting links to articles she has written on her OMP. For example, this week she might write an article on how three students in her Yoga class have been attending every session for the last six months straight. She might include a photo of the class, or just those three members in Sphinx Pose. This is a callout to the community, just like "Nate", the musician did in our original example of the right way to handle social media. This entire article might take 10 minutes to create and post, and then share the link on Facebook. But the value of something like this is extraordinary. Think about what is communicated in a post like this:

- We are a happy place
- We have long term customers
- We have loyal customers
- We have satisfied customers
- These are women who look just like you
- We celebrate our successes

The implicit message is an invitation to share in that success. The members you pictured in the article will go onto Facebook and share the photo with their friends and family. Suddenly, what was an article on your platform has now reached over a thousand people, without you spending a dime in advertising.

And that's just one article. The second article in the week should be something that showcases your knowledge about your product or service. If you are a Yoga instructor, perhaps a quick article on increasing flexibility. If you are an insurance agent, an article on the importance of calling your agent before you call the claims department might be a good topic. A chiropractor might talk about how he uses a specific combination of tools and treatments to relieve TMJ in his practice. Regardless of the field you are in, you can find one subject a week to discuss. Even a flooring installer can talk about the different kinds of adhesives that should be used for different kinds of flooring and subsurfaces. It doesn't matter. All it has to do is showcase your expertise.

And then you post it on your OMP, then post the link to it on Facebook. Don't expect any great response from this one because people will be sharing it wildly, but you need to put it out there for people to find. Or, more correctly, for you to find people. As with most things you post, it is actually a kind of "bait" to attract people who are exactly in your target audience. If you can get these people, even in low numbers, to go to your OMP, then you have succeeded in bringing them into your online showroom. But now, it's time to engage them in conversation, even if they never tell you their names.

Retargeting

In the last few years, an incredibly new tool has become available for small businesses. This tool, called retargeting, allows OMP owners to "tag" people who have visited viewed their content online, and then report that tag back to a central database. Then, if the OMP owner chooses, she can retarget those visitors with ads and announcements in the future. If you're having trouble with that explanation, try this analogy.

Imagine you owned a specialty clothing store in the mall, and you target young, professional men. Clearly not every person who comes into the mall is your target customer, but just about everyone that stops and looks at your window, or comes into your store, is a good prospect for a future sale. What if you could get smart phone number of every person who stopped by, regardless of whether they filled out a form or even spoke to a sales associate in your store? What if just the act of stopping to look in your store activated an app on their phone allowed you to send them text messages later on to tell them about sales or special events, and there was virtually nothing they could do to stop it? And, in fact, once they got over the privacy issue, they realized it was actually helping them by giving them information they really wanted, regardless of whether they even asked for it?

That's what retargeting does, and at this point, nobody allows you to do it better, or easier, than Facebook.

You've been out to websites where they ask you to join their mailing lists? Maybe one in a hundred actually does that. But with retargeting, you can put a piece of code into the header of each page in your website, and whenever anybody with an active Facebook account visits any page in your site, Facebook logs that visit, and adds their Facebook ID to a lockbox with your name on it. Depending upon how many of your visitors have Facebook accounts, that capture ratio could approach 100%. You never get to see who the individual visitors are, but Facebook puts them aside for you, and then you can send ads directly to those people, and if you have enough, to those people only.

But now, take it one step further. If you are using Facebook to drive your traffic to your site, then 100% of those visitors will definitely have a Facebook account. Everyone who reads your message on Facebook and decides to visit your site will become a captured lead for you. This is why it is important to have those "expert articles" appearing every week on your site. They are creating a steady stream of newly minted prospects directly into your Facebook retargeting database. Depending upon the amount of traffic you generate, you can tell Facebook to keep people in that list for up to six months, before it moves them out. Naturally, whenever they visit again, they will be re-added to the list, and the six month period will start again. If you are getting tens of thousands of visitors a month, however, you may not have a sufficient ad budget to be targeting all of them, and you may choose to only keep leads alive for two months or four months. This will also depend upon your sales cycle.

So let's put this entire social media thing back into perspective, because although we started with a very strong statement about it NOT being advertising and media, we have ended with what appears to be a very technical, almost mercenary approach to our management of the resource.

Your first focus in social media should always be on "social". Media is just how it happens. Your personal account on Facebook should be exactly that: personal. You have to be a real person, and who you really are. If you are a raging animal rights activist, don't hide it on your personal page because you might offend a customer. Anybody who gets to know you is probably going to find it out sooner or later, anyway. When you try to hide it, though, you end up sounding like you're, well, hiding something. As the old saying goes, people don't buy from companies, they buy from people. You need to be a real person, and real people have opinions on issues.

You don't have to proselytize from your Facebook pulpit about whether the Humane Society uses its donations appropriately, but it doesn't hurt for you to be sharing articles or commenting on them in a professional manner, either. In fact, what ends up happening is people feel more comfortable buying from someone who genuinely shares their beliefs or opinions on subjects, and it can cause MORE people to buy from you than it would cause people to avoid you.

And, in fact, Facebook makes it very easy to decide who can and can't see your posts. Personally, I keep everything set to "public", so anybody who wants to see who I really am can just go right to my wall, whether they have friend requested me or not, and find out what I think, feel and believe about subjects. This is an honest public persona, and you know it is because it has been consistent for years and years. People can see that I politely handle those who disagree with my positions, and I fervidly defend those who share them. That's who I am, and if you have had even a modicum of honest success in business, that's probably who you are, too. People can find pictures of my family, my vacation trips, my animals, and occasionally, amidst all that reality, they can also find brief references to my work.

Contrast this with a local businessman I follow on Facebook named "Charlie". Charlie posts pictures of beautiful women in seductive poses… and ads for his business. That's it. Except for an occasional, "Happy Memorial Day" type post, that's all he posts. Are we really to believe there is nothing more of Charlie? Or, more likely, is he afraid people will find out who he really is, and then not buy his product? And if Charlie, who knows Charlie the best, knows that he is the kind of person that would turn off customers, shouldn't we believe him and just not do business with him?

Yes, that IS how the human mind works, and how people actually view your presence on Social Media. Because they can't see your face, or observe your body language, or note your manner of dress, they can only assess you based upon what you present to the public. Make it a complete, well rounded picture of yourself, and then be the professional your business needs you to be.

Let's recap the entire social media process now, to make sure you have an easy map to follow.

1. Create a weekly article on your OMP highlighting your expertise in your business, recounting how you solved a customer issue, or discussing an important "how to" so people can get valuable information from your Online Marketing Platform.

2. Post that article to your Facebook Business Page. Make sure it has a professional image attached so that it shows up whenever anyone shares the article on their own wall. (This is called a "featured image" in both WordPress and DRIVOR sites)

3. Create a second post every week simply highlighting events that happened in your store, happy customers, or something that gives the correct impression of how people who do

business with you FEEL about your business. The optimum results are achieved when you create a new post every day, but just one a day. That has been shown to be the best trigger for the algorithm. Do the best you can. The maximum target isn't that far from the minimum effort.

4. Create an ad that targets your followers (and retargeting site visitors, if you have that set up) by letting them know you have written a new article (the one in step 1) and they can read it by included the link.

5. Maintain regular activity on your personal page. Engage with friends and family. Be real.

6. GIVE at least 4 articles that help others before you ASK them to do anything for you. So if it takes you four weeks to create four articles that teach people how to garden, you have to wait until the FIFTH week to ask them to check out the new rose bushes you have on sale. Giving is 80% of what you do in social media. Asking for people to consider you for their next purchase is just 20% of your messaging. The most successful marketers do even less than that. Some have reached zero percent, because their OMP moves them into a sales process, thus their social media can be used exclusively to attract visitors with the warm and fuzzies.

7. Don't be afraid to share information that is not on your own OMP, but try to keep it to a minimum. Be a useful resource to your potential customers.

If you make it all about you, that can also turn others off. If a competitor in another state writes a great blog article, then share it. You're not going to lose business over it, but the fact that you are confident enough to share competitor's material says a lot about you and the strength of your business. People gravitate to success. Use that to your advantage.

Having said that, there are a lot of people out there who use other people's material as a springboard for their own articles and posts. If you see someone else's article that leaves out important information, then by all means write ABOUT that other article, QUOTE that other article, and then provide a LINK to that article... on your own blog! Don't just comment on it in on Facebook if your comment has real significance. Own that turf and bring people to it.

8. Rinse and repeat.

That's your simple cycle for social media. Believe it or not, you can do all that in less than an hour a week. Sure, your personal stuff will take more time, but you're probably going to do that anyway. And so what if amongst the pictures of your new puppy and your kid's graduation, you also have a post that says, "Hey, I just wrote this article on changing your bicycle chain. Have a look!", who cares? People will remember that bicycles are your business, and some of your friends may share the article and get you a referral. If your business is a part of your life, then you also shouldn't hide that in your social media presence, either. Just don't make it the only thing you talk about. X might work that way, because people on X choose whom they follow based on interests, not on life. But Facebook is about the WHOLE you. That is why Facebook is winning the social media war, because it's about the "social", not about the "media".

Tips for Facebook Business Pages

In the same way your Online Marketing Platform is the hub of all your online marketing activity, your Facebook Business Page should be the hub of all your Facebook business activity. What I'm going to discuss here are the "best practices" for managing your page so that you get the most impact for your effort. I'd say "bang for your buck", but most of what we'll be discussing here doesn't cost you anything but a few minutes of your time every day. Don't think of social media as a chore or task. It's not like you're going out in 92^0 heat to hold up signs in the median of a highway. What you're doing is talking to your customers. When a customer walks into your store, you don't pounce on them and start blathering on about your overstocked water heaters. Your $9 an hour cashier might do that, but that's not how you would handle real customer who graced you with their presence. Instead, you would engage them in dialogue, find out what they need, and then discuss their options with them. Perhaps your overstocked water heater is just right. Or perhaps they are looking to buy all new appliances for their entire household. You don't know until you ask.

NOTE: I won't be giving explicit, step by step instructions on how to do these things on Facebook, and that's because by the time you read this, some of those steps will have changed. All internet based technology is subject to RAPID change without notice. You wake up one morning, and the internet gods have decided you needed to get rid of that dashboard you've used for three years and replace it with a new cPanel that they assure you will make your life "easier". (True story: I had a special exemption from Godaddy that kept my old dashboard in place, rather than replacing it with the new control panel they had been giving to every new customer for a couple years. I frequently did specific tasks in one step that simply weren't available as a single step option in the new panel. Well, after a year or two, they MADE it functional, and so I made the complete switch.) So the best thing for you to do is take what I'm telling you, then either search the "help" files on Facebook for how to do it, or check out my site WeCraftSites.com to find the latest technical updates on how to do those little things that keep moving around.

Boosting versus Ads

Boosting is not advertising, and advertising is not boosting.

I used to suggest doing a combination of the two. Now, I have fallen into the "NeverBoost" camp, and I'll explain why.

Boosting is a quick fix that shoots out to everyone immediately. Although that might sound appealing, it means that the discernment of your best customers suffers in exchange for the quick fix of views. Facebook will shove your post in front of anybody that even remotely fits the requirement you set… sometimes multiple times, if they can't find anybody else in the first 24 hours. That gets real old real fast.

The fact is, though, that Boosting actually costs you about FOUR TIMES as much as just running the exact same content as an ad. It's basically an impulse-aisle product designed to make it "easy" to spend your money… and getting you whatever response you might get, if any. So don't fall for it. Take a few extra minutes and get four times the results for the same dollar spent. Set yourself up with an ad that targets your page followers (and people who are like them) and let that run for 3 days. Instead of spending $6 on day one, spend $2 on each day and you should see a pronounced difference in your return.

Straight up advertising is different, though. With advertising you are seeking to attract new people to become followers of your page, your OMP and

111

ultimately, your business. This is the reliable source of fresh leads from your community, so you have to think carefully about the demographics and psychographics of your customers to decide the people you wish to spend money attracting.

Within the "Create Ad" part of Facebook, you can narrow down your target demographics by age, gender, and most importantly, geography. If you have a restaurant, there's no point in advertising to people more than 25 miles away. Don't waste the money trying to draw people from two towns over just because somebody over there came in once and loved the place. If you have a group of people in distant places they will hopefully be following your page, and you will get your message to them and their friends by boosting. Don't waste advertising dollars on them. Having said that, Facebook has added a new feature for finding people who are "just passing through" your area. This is a goldmine for restaurants and attractions that rely on people who don't know the community and might be wanting lunch or drinks or axe throwing!

Once you've decided on your geographic settings, you can then get around to deciding what kind of people you are seeking. You can narrow the numbers down by age and by gender. Clearly, if you are running a gym for ladies only, you aren't going to bother spending money advertising to men. (Not only will they not buy from you, but no man is going to take the risk of suggesting his wife needs to get a gym membership! On the other hand, you can probably create quite a campaign for a men's gym by targeting their wives!)

Age settings are as specific as you want them to be. Imagine creating an ad for women who were 47 to 49 years old, with a headline, "Getting (uncomfortably) close to 50?". This is an excellent example of how tightly you can market your business on Facebook. Now watch how we make it even tighter by finding the psychographics that match your model customer.

Psychographic Marketing on Facebook

When it comes to psychographics, nobody compares to Facebook. Because they have such a huge percentage of the population in their database, they can slice and dice them based on the tiniest sliver of interests, occupations or even political beliefs. If you're advertising a gun shop, finding people who have expressed an interest in the Second Amendment is probably a great place to advertise your "Concealed Carry" class starting this Saturday. I have worked with businesses in the equestrian industry who have found literally thousands of potential customers within a few dozen miles of their stores, and they market to them relentlessly. Their Facebook following has exploded… and so have their floor traffic and sales. These people are right there around your store, but they need to know about you if they are going to consider you when making their next purchase. Facebook advertising lets you find them, converse with them, and eventually invite them to shop with you.

And if you are a recruiter, or you have a business that focuses on a large local employer, you have the capability to target people by their place of employment. First, you create the audience that lists your target business as their employer, and then you aim your ads at that audience. If you've been parking your lunch truck outside Lockheed Martin's offices for six months with limited success, maybe you should consider creating an ad on Facebook that lets them know what is on your menu, what your hours are that you will be parked in front of their building, and what your daily special is. You can probably hit a large percentage of the employees who would never consider you an option before seeing your ad. Why wait for word of mouth? Create it!

There are about a thousand courses and videos on how to create successful Facebook ads. The problem is, most of them are designed around the idea of internet marketing, not around business marketing online. You don't need to be quite as aggressive as they are, but you can use the ad to offer specials or deals to anyone who clicks on the link. This can take them to your OMP where they can register and get an introductory coupon for a free drink, a free round of golf, or a 50% discount on their first chair massage.

Again, your budget only needs to be between $1 and $5 a day. The equestrian store I previously mentioned had a total budget of $1 a day ($22 a month) for all their Facebook advertising. And it worked.

Play with it

Nothing you do is the best you can do. Time changes everything. And that's good. Your ads on Facebook can't be compared to anybody else's ads because they aren't in your business in your town with your customers. You have to start keeping track of what your ads are doing, how effective they are at driving traffic and new fans to your page, and ultimately, how much money they spend with you. This is actually the REAL work of online marketing. When you create an ad, you can create multiple cover images. Facebook will change those images for you automatically, (this is called A/B Split Testing) and then you can see which image gets more attention. You then dump the image that isn't doing as well, and immediately add ANOTHER image in its place. Then you compare these two images for performance. Whichever one gets better response is kept, and the other is replaced. You never stop improving your performance.

Seriously, why would you spend $22 a month to get five new customers when you can spend the same $22 and get seven? Or nine? You won't know how much better you could be doing until you try, and Facebook allows you to do this split testing all day long on every campaign. You don't need to go crazy with this, but remember to use this system to find out what you can be doing better.

In fact, the cover picture for your ad is just the easy change. You can actually create ads with different headlines, body copy, call to action buttons… every detail can be tweaked to see how it affects your response. The key to good split testing (or A/B testing, as it is currently labeled in the Facebook Ads Manager) is to only change ONE element at a time. If you change more than one, you won't know which change caused the difference in response, or if one negative change actually cancelled out another positive one in the same ad. One variable at a time. It's a marathon, not a sprint.

There is another setting that can really help you improve performance, and that has to do with the timing of your ad. You can set your ads to only appear at certain times of the day. So, if you are having a big event starting at 3:00 PM, you can have different ad campaigns running on the days leading up to the event, and then different ads running right up TO the event. Imagine seeing "Happy Hour starts in less than an hour!" on your Facebook wall. It gives you urgency, and because the timeframe is so tight, you can spread your advertising dollars over a wider swath of the market. By focusing on the exact time window, you can expand the number of people who see your message in that tight timeframe. This is great for business. We used this kind of "time based" marketing for a political campaign on election day, and it worked brilliantly. If you have a special that ends today, you can almost give people a countdown to the time you close and the deals go away.

This system has been used very successfully by internet marketers to get people to sign up for their webinars, but there's no reason you can't adapt it to get your customers into your "live" events. It's easy to set up and once done, it is entirely automated. All you have to do is plan your work a little bit in advance and you can begin to see excellent results. This system works well because it gives a sense of urgency to your message. Sometimes this urgency can be the emotional energy needed to get people over the hump of stagnancy momentum. A body in motion stays in motion; a body at rest stays at rest. You need to get their resting body in motion. An urgency campaign might be just the trick to do it.

Those are the basic elements of handling Facebook for your social media marketing. Allow me to recap them here, in bullet form:

- Be sincere, genuine and honest. Facebook is about PEOPLE, not about messages. Unless people feel that you are sincerely interested in them, they aren't going to see your business as anything but an empty husk.

- It's okay to have opinions. That's part of being real. Don't be over the top, unless you are sure you have a small segment of your audience that will absolutely LOVE your position, and become better, more faithful customers (and evangelists) because of it. I'm not advising you become a populist; just don't be afraid to be you.

- Be reliable. Post consistently. Try to have at least one message up every day.

- Have one good content piece created on your OMP every week, and share that on your FB wall. Boost that piece so that as many of your fans and followers can see it. That's why they signed up. Because it has an external link, Facebook won't show it to as many people as a plain image post. That doesn't matter. You have a plan, so stick with it.

- Capture life moments with a picture or video and put that up on your Business Page. If an employee is working extra hard, catch 'em in the act. If a customer is especially happy with something you did, ask them to smile for the camera. If it's going to take more than 30 words to explain it, then turn it into a site post and drive the traffic back to your OMP.

- Create regular ad campaigns to attract new customers.

- Split test all your ad campaigns. Constantly be improving.

- Target your audience geographically, demographically and psychographically. The more you narrow down the market and the message, the higher your response rate will be.

- Spend your money sparingly. See what two dollars a day gets you. If you are running your split testing regularly, you will always be creating new versions of your ads. Once in a while, though, create something entirely different. Run it simultaneously against your standard ad. You may get a pleasant surprise. Let your real life customers inspire you.

Other Social Media Channels

So now that you understand all that about Facebook, and you have got the system down pat and you are running it regularly and know what it will get you... THEN you can perhaps look at adding another social media channel. Now that you are practiced at creating messages, updating information on a regular basis, and tracking the results of those messages, you have a benchmark against which you can compare the new social media channel. If you have good customers always talking about stuff on Instagram, then perhaps that might be a place where you can find more customers like them. But until you master one channel, you won't know what is good or bad on the other. It's just like split testing your ads. Let Facebook be your benchmark, and judge the other channels from there.

LinkedIn

I get asked a lot about LinkedIn, especially by my B2B customers. I'm going to give it special attention, because I think many people are having questions about it right now.

LinkedIn has evolved a LOT since I wrote the first draft of this book. It used to be that all your contacts had their emails available and you could just download them in a spreadsheet form. What a quick way to grow your email list!

Well, those days are long gone. Now, LinkedIn is an important place to have a professional presence and discuss elements important to your business, but realize it is little more than a fruitless B2B sales channel, where everybody is trying to sell everybody else the same things they are trying to sell … to everybody else. It's like Amway: People go there to sell stuff, never to buy anything themselves. Having said that, you should maintain your corporate "presence" on the channel, because people have traditionally seen it as a much more reputable source of business background information than a Facebook Business Page, but that is changing fast. You can do both, but make LinkedIn a simple billboard for your business. Drive them back to your website for questions. Your content marketing can also be posted there, and who knows? You might actually generate a legitimate lead or two.

The Fourth Driver

Email

What is the most valuable asset your company can own? If you thought it was your inventory, your bank account, or your employees, you are wrong.

It is your email list. Your email list is something you can turn to in a split second to create immediate revenue for your business. If you have a surprise repair bill come up, you can instantly send out an email announcing a special sale on certain products and get people in the door (or onto your e-commerce platform) in seconds. If you have customers, you can find a product for them. Heck, you can even ask them to pre-order a product you don't even have in stock yet! You can't do this with any other business asset. Nothing even comes close.

Before we get into a serious discussion about email marketing, we first have to get you over the emotional hump of spam. Here's a quick way to do that. Picture this: A new friend asks you to send him an email to remind him of a dinner you're having with a group of friends on Saturday night. He then gives you his email address so you can send him the restaurant details.

Would you consider that spamming your new friend? Of course not. He wants to know where you are supposed to meet. In fact, he'll feel disappointed and neglected if you don't send it. He might miss the dinner, and that will leave him frustrated with you. He believes that the content of that email is valuable, and therefore he wants to receive it.

And that, dear reader, is the core of good email marketing. The emails you send to your customers (or prospective customers) have to contain the exact, valuable information they expect to receive from you when they give you their email address. You tell them what you are going to email them, and then you email it to them. I'm afraid that's as complicated as it gets. But if you violate that simple rule, you are spamming people. Period.

That is also how you build your email list. One person, one individual, at a time. I have added hundreds of people to my email list, simply by asking them to be on it when they hand me their business cards. A face to face enrollment is an awesome way to get people on your email list, and it also reminds you of the sanctity of the agreement you are making with them when they say, "Sure, add me to it!". If you have read and emotionally internalized what I have written here, then you will know exactly where this next section is headed.

Buying Email Lists

There are dozens of services out there who will sell you email lists. You can get hundreds, even thousands of names and email addresses for pennies apiece. They'll tell you how "fresh" they are, how "active" they are, how "responsive" they are.

And the answer is always "no". Not just "no", really, but "Hell no!".

These people on this list are not your fans, your friends, or your followers. They have no idea who you are. And their first impression of you will be that you are the kind of person who will trespass in their email inbox, and violate their privacy. They will always view you with a level of distrust, because they don't know how you found them. That's how scammers work. You shouldn't be using the same tactics as identity thieves and phishers. As we go through the process of how to use your email marketing to build your business, you will understand why this is more important than ever.

Creating your list

For the purposes of modern marketing online, it is crucial that you understand this simple truth: It is better to have five people on your email list that asked to be there than it is to have 500 who didn't ask, don't know you, and have no idea what you do for work. Knowing this does a few things:

1. It keeps your list clean

2. It keeps you clear from violating CAN/ SPAMM rules

3. It keeps your metrics tight and meaningful

4. It takes the pressure off of you thinking you have to have a huge list.

So, now that the pressure is off, we can explore simple, effective ways of growing your email list organically. No tricks, no schemes, no bait and switch tactics.

Current Contacts

Right below asking people in person if you can add them to your list is an old trick that can really buff up your mailing list pretty fast. It's your own Rolodex. Obviously you already have prospective customers in mind, but in order to do this right, you need to follow a two step process. I know a business owner who actually got burned on this one, and I don't want you to make the same mistake.

Go through your old business cards and start pulling names and email addresses from them. Do not, however, assume that they want to be on your regular email list. (This is where the business owner got burned). You must create a second list for these people, and you must first ASK them if they wouldn't mind receiving occasional updates and offers from you. Below is an example of the kind of letter you might send to this list. Obviously, you need to use your own "voice" when writing your email. Keep it friendly and personal. You are the only one who knows how many people are receiving it.

Kevin,

I'm wondering if you wouldn't mind giving me a hand with a project. Your part is easy. I'm going to be putting out a couple articles soon, and

I'd like your permission to send them to you to get your thoughts on them. Occasionally I might forward along other information as well, but it all comes from me, not some email service.

If I don't hear back from you, I'll just go ahead with the plan. If you have any questions, of course you can email me back by hitting "reply". And, if you don't want to look over this information from me, then just reply and say "No thanks".

I appreciate your help.

Jane

Notice I haven't asked them if they want to receive spam from me. That's how a human interprets "add your personal information to another email list" if you aren't there in person to humanize the request. It's really important that you keep all communication very personal. It's also really important that you make the "opt in" the easiest option for them. That's why a "no reply" is considered an opt in for this part of the campaign. These are people you know. And, because they are people you know, very few of them will confront you with a "No thanks". And those that do simply aren't your best prospects for your email campaign, so it is no loss to you.

Business Cards

This is perhaps the easiest trick that I've used over the years, and has resulted in me growing my list pretty effectively. It's simple, really. Whenever you go to a mixer, networking event or trade show, just be sure to ask people that you meet if it is all right if you add them to your email list. To date, I have never had anyone say "no" to this request. Obviously, you are not there to gather leads for your email campaign, but when you meet someone who may be a good prospect for what you do, but isn't ready to buy at that exact moment, it is a great idea to keep them aware of you by sending them regular emails about your business. We will discuss email content in a later section, but the bottom line is, you can probably add one or two people a week using this method. In a couple weeks, you'll have your first five people.

Passive Opt In

Since you now have an awesome Online Marketing Platform, there is no reason you shouldn't have a simple form where people can leave their names and email addresses so that they can voluntarily receive more information from you as it becomes available.

Something as simple as this can get you a few responses, based on the amount of traffic you are driving to your site:

Want to receive updates from us? Stop working so hard and let us just send them to you!

There are several ways to do it, but the fact is that about 60% of opt ins come from an offer for a discount or coupon. So, if you want to get the highest opt-in rate for your business, consider a message like this:

Looking for discounts and coupons? Sign up here to get them delivered to your inbox!

The first message is passive, with very little benefit. The second one promises discounts and coupons, so if you are in a business that offers these kinds of promotions, you can use them to your advantage in this way.

Active Opt In

The Active Opt In requires some more time and effort on your part, but it is the number one way of gathering focused leads on the internet. In order to make this one work, you have to be actively offering something of value in exchange for them giving you their email address. The trick to this is making the "something of value" directly related to the kind of customer you are seeking to acquire for your mailing list. Let me explain by example.

You are Vicky and you run a Personal Injury law firm. Which of these two offers is going to help you grow your business?

1. Sign up now and we'll give you a FREE "Vicky's Law Firm" coffee mug!

2. Give us your email address and we'll send you our FREE report, "Five Things to Do in the First Five Days after a Car Accident"

The first offer is going to attract people who want a free coffee mug. Gee. That's everybody. (My friend Alex will probably use ten different email addresses to get ten mugs, because he loves coffee that much.) The second one, however, is going to only attract people who have been in a car accident recently, and want to find out what to do, or if what they did was the right thing. Either way, you have a list that is filled almost exclusively with people who have been in car accidents. (Attorneys understand that many people will SWITCH attorneys during the course of their litigation, so even if they've already signed on with someone, they can still be a good prospect for a switchover.)

Therefore, creating the right offer piece is of paramount importance. Don't be so in love with what you think your customers want that you don't give them any other options, either. Sometimes a subtle change in the title can make a 50% difference in the effectiveness of your list gathering program. I can tell you this, and it is both from experience and hard statistics: Keep it simple, and make sure it's a "numbered list offer". Again, to make sure you understand this, here are two headlines. The second one is the right one.

1. The Legal Process After an Accident: What Every Victim Must Understand Before Going to Court

2. Four Things you MUST Do Within 72 hours of Your Accident

People are inherently lazy, and they want to know that what they are committing to when reading this. They are far more likely to open the article if they know upfront that it isn't going to be the equivalent of reading Victor Hugo or a Master's thesis.

So think about what your customers already ask you, and then imagine that there are hundreds of new customers out there who would also like to know the answer to that same question. Offering people a list of things they need to know is one of the best things you can do to attract your target customers or clients to your business. If you own an insurance agency, and you want to attract new people for homeowners insurance, then put out a piece on what is and is not covered when you have a flood. If you want to attract automobile insurance customers, then create a page on how to keep your insurance premiums low when buying car insurance. Target the piece at the market you want to attract.

And then let it go to work.

If you have a good system in place, then whenever anybody replies to your request for an email address, they will instantly be directed to a page where they can download the document, or it can be emailed directly to them. All of this happens automatically now, so you can have your Marketing Platform working all kinds of crazy hours, and never have to pay overtime. You give the gift, and then wait for the thank you card to arrive. Except, actually, you are getting the thank you card (the contact information) before they get the gift.

Regardless of how you deliver it, the "gift" you are offering can be directly tailored to the needs of the clients you want to attract. You can create these documents in Microsoft Word or Apple Pages, then simply save them as a PDF. Remember, though, it's not so much about the appearance of the page as it is about the quality of the content. You can really showcase your expertise, and help people learn to rely on you, by giving them something truly valuable in this offer.

And then, as soon as you have this system up and running smoothly, generating leads for your business, then it's time to sit back and…. create another one. Every few weeks it's a good idea to make a new offer to your prospective customers. It doesn't take much effort once you've done two or three of them to simply keep cranking out useful pieces of advice or experience for your prospects. Here is a list of some quick prompts for you to get going, though:

- Three things you never knew about_____.

- Five things you need to do before you
  _____.

- Do these four things and you won't have
  problems with your_____.

- Suffering from _____? Here's how you
  fix it fast!

- Four things other people did to make their
  _____ better.

- Older _____? How to know when
  to Repair or Replace.

- How to care for your new _____.
  Six things you should be doing right now.

- Save money on your _____ repair by
  doing these things FIRST!

The point is, you have to be in a constant state of giving. But unlike the samples you might give to a customer who walks in the door, these only cost you a bit of time to create one, then they can duplicate themselves ad infinitum. There will always be just one more free sample for the next customer who wants one.

Email Content

Of course, now that you have an email list, that's just the beginning. Your next job is to fill that email with things these people might appreciate receiving. If you have a DRIVOR™ site, then you already know where a lot of your email content comes from. If not, then allow me to give you some ideas that you can employ to give you things to send to your prospects every week.

Newsletter

The newsletter format is popular because it gives people a smattering of all the areas of your business in one location. Consider including one original article (perhaps a monthly summary of events and circumstances that affected the business), as well as upcoming events and specials that people won't want to miss. Some people do weekly newsletters, and as you grow, you may find that to be an important part of your marketing program. At the minimum, though, you should publish one monthly.

Write Articles

Obviously, the absolutely best thing you can do is write an article or two every week, just for your newsletter recipients. Between writing and editing, you should consider setting aside an hour or two for this task alone. Regardless of the time consumption, this is the best way to make sure your email directly reflects the latest, most important things going on in your business, according to your perspective. And that's why people asked to be on your list, remember?

Coupons and Discounts (Don't be Rosetta Stone)

These are also really good things to send out on a regular basis, as people will train themselves to open your emails just to see what they might get a discount on this week. Make sure you make these coupons valuable, and that you change them up every time you send one. There's nothing worse than a stale offer, repeated ad nauseum. The best example I have of this is the daily email I get from the language software company, Rosetta Stone. Every two days I get an email proclaiming that THIS is their biggest sale of the year, and I'm going to miss it. The headline changes a little bit every time, but the offer is always within $10 (out of $500) of the same price ($299) day in, day out. Week after week. Month after month. YEAR AFTER YEAR! They've not only lost the sense of urgency that might compel me to buy their course, but honestly they've become a household joke, as my wife gets the same emails from them.

If you're in a service business, it might be hard to come up with offers that change regularly. For example, if you're a chiropractor or an attorney, you may always have a free initial consultation/treatment, because that's really all the law will allow you to do. In that case, you won't be sending out a sheet of coupons, but you might always put a coupon/offer at the bottom of your content based emails, and put a note on it about sharing it with others who might need it right now.

Site Content

The easiest source of material, however, is your own OMP. That article you wrote and posted on your site is your quickest, easiest material to grab and put in an email. Also, if structured correctly, it can serve another purpose: drive people back to your OMP where you can control the conversation. That's the whole point to all of this, anyway, remember?

To do this, all you need to do is copy/paste your article into an email and send it out. Poof. Done for the week. There are two schools of thought on how to do this, however, and I'll give you both of them and let you discover which one works better for your particular business.

1. Include the title and an excerpt from your blog post, then a link to the full article where they can finish reading it.

2. Include the entire article, but give them strong prompts to share it themselves in social media, or by forwarding the email to friends. Seth Godin does this, and I suppose it works well for him because, honestly, he isn't selling anything. He's just a key person of influence and people want to hear what he has to say on various subjects.

I think the first one works better for small businesses. Your goal is to bring people to your site so you can give them the full business experience. It's not about giving them the content of one article, but rather about making sure they understand the full fleet of products and services you offer. However you do it, remember that once your list gets big enough, you can do the same kind of split testing that you did with social media advertising. In order to do that, though, you need to sign up with an actual email service. Allow me to discuss my old standby: MailChimp.

MailChimp

Mailchimp is an email service that allows you to build your email marketing program for free. Their business model is simple: let you build your list there (up to 2,000 people) and send up to 12,000 emails a month, so that when you get bigger and need more, you will choose their service over all the others. And frankly, their service is pretty darned good. You can put your contacts into a spreadsheet and then just upload them to MailChimp. You can add people one at a time. When you add a person, you can ask MailChimp to verify that they aren't already on your list, thus avoiding duplication. And unlike sending bulk emails from your personal account, you won't accidentally display all 78 email names and addresses of the recipients by putting the names in the "To" box instead of the "BCC" box.

When you use MailChimp, you also get the wonderful bonus of a full LIVE report as your email is delivered to your recipients. You will know how many went to bad addresses, how many were opened, and most importantly, how many people clicked on the links in your email. And then, even more importantly, MailChimp will tell you exactly WHO clicked on the links. Imagine seeing that Jane McSmith read your article on potting soil for roses. The next time she comes in the store, you might ask her if she saw the article on potting soil for roses (of course, you know she did), and perhaps find out that she was planning on putting in a dozen new rose bushes, but was ready to buy them somewhere else. How could you turn that conversation into a big sale?

Okay, is that like "creepy spying"? Not really. Imagine you had brochures around your showroom, and somebody picked up the one on potting soil for roses. Is it "creepy spying" to notice this and comment on it? Of course not. It's perhaps the best opener you can use for a sales conversation, and you shouldn't take away that ability just because it's been automated.

The really good thing about the email metrics provided by MailChimp is that you can start to get a good feel for what kind of email subject lines cause your prospects to open your emails. Is it "We now have Bunny Rabbits", or "See the Baby Bunnies we have in stock right now! (Photos enclosed)". By keeping track of this, and then by seeing which links are clicked on most frequently within your email (yes, it also tracks those separately), you can keep refining your article titles and email headlines to get the most out of your program. You should spend time every week reviewing your metrics and tweaking your program to improve the response.

Monthly Process
I suggest the following regular monthly process for your email program.

Week 1: Send a copy of a blog post

Week 2: Blog post with special offer

Week 3: Copy of a blog post

Week 4: NEWSLETTER, including titles/excerpts from your blog posts, plus offers, plus one original article that you or a member of your staff puts together. If you have a popular employee who wants to be a writer, then this is their big break!

And that's your monthly email program. Rinse and repeat.

A note about DRIVOR™ : If you have a classic DRIVOR site, then you already have this self-driving functionality built in. All email addresses gathered by your OMP are automatically added to your mailing list, and then all your site articles are automatically published as emails weekly. All you have to do is focus on your monthly newsletter article. The rest of the content of your newsletter is generated automatically by the DRIVOR™ software.

However, in recent months I have been moving away from Mailchimp and using a Customer Relationship Management (CRM) program that is built right into the back end of your OMP. This program adds much of the functionality of Mailchimp, but gives you complete ownership of the entire process.

In a world where services are cancelling people because of the products they sell, or the company they keep, it is a good idea to keep control of your most valuable assets.

The Fifth Driver

Multi-Media

Up to this point, we have mostly discussed the creation of written content for your site content. Although words can allow us to be precise in our communication, they are not the only tools we have at our disposal for communicating our message to our prospective customers. In this section, we will examine some of the other methods we have for communicating our business messages, as well as inexpesive (or free!) tools you can use to create some pretty high quality material to put on your OMP.

Before we do that, let's make sure you have a firm foundation in WHY you need to be using multi-media to communicate your ideas. In order to do that, we must first understand what I mean when I say "multi-media".

Multi-Media Marketing: The use of different media to communicate an idea, thought or concept to a prospective customer. This may include any combination of the following:

- Photographs

- Clipart

- Infographics

- Audio recordings (podcasts)

- GIF images

- Animated videos

- Voice Over Image Video

- Action video

- Studio video

You have lots of options for how you can communicate your message, and you should use far more than one of them if you want to get a really good return on your marketing efforts. We'll start by discussing the easiest ones, and then move up to the more complicated pieces to create. You have to remember, though, that the further you go down the list, usually the better the response you get for your effort, and the better ROI you get for your marketing budget.

Photographs

Photographs are just that: pictures of people or things that relate to your business. Within the category of Photographs, there are two sub-categories: Custom photos and Stock photos. Both can be used very easily, but I will say right now that when dealing with social media and your current customers, you will get a better response from Custom photos than you will from stock photos.

A Custom photo is one you take yourself (or someone on your staff takes). It shows a specific item, people or activity that may or may not directly relate to your business. The fact is, you clicked the button. This is different from a Stock photo, in which someone else has provided you with an image that you, and just about anybody else in the world, can use as described in a licensing agreement. Not every photo you see on a Google Image search is free for you to grab and stick on your blog! However, there are some GREAT sources for free images, and I'll be listing those in the "Resource" section in the book. Some of the ones I like are Pixabay, Pexel, and FreeImages. All of these services offer you the use of their images for free, after you create an account on their sites. Honestly, I don't ever get email from them, even though I've had accounts for a very long time. It's painless, and the rewards are outstanding. These sites have hundreds of thousands of images available, and are still growing fast. You simply input your key word (Like "canoe") and you'll get back all the images they have with "canoe" in the key word description.

A word of caution: All of these sites make their money by teasing you with their free content, but hoping you will click on the NOT free images at the top of the page. If you see the perfect image in that Sponsored section of their catalog, then you can expect to pay between $20 and $400 to use those pictures. For what you'll be doing with these, you can almost always make do with the free images on the lower part of the page.

When you are using your own Custom photos, you also need to make sure that anyone who is identifiably appearing in those pictures has given you permission to use them. Have a stack of Release forms by your counter for when customers come in and you want to take their picture with their new purchase. You must have this, unless the people you are photographing are outside, in public. Most states exempt privacy for people in public, but I'm not a lawyer, and this isn't legal advice. If you are going to do a lot of photography, check with your professional advisor.

Custom Photographs

Take and use custom photographs with your phone. Get in the habit of taking them a lot. Download them onto your laptop/desktop computer, or into an online folder in Dropbox, if you have to, but don't be afraid to take a picture of a nice piece of yard work you did for a customer, or a beautiful fruit basket you are sending to a retiring client, or your manufacturing line making custom parts for incinerators, or a client with a new hair color she just loves. All of these are about your business and what it does, how it does it, and every one of these images tells a story. Be sure your picture is part of a story that you can "round out" with a few dozen words. Showing a happy customer tells people the important things they really want to know about your business. Showing happy workers, or a cheerful work environment, helps people to feel good about giving you their money because they feel like it's going to be used properly. (In contrast, don't show a picture of your Jacuzzi/swimming pool combo with your new Porsche parked in the distance and then claim you can't lower your prices to compete with the Box Stores. Remember, social media requires honest transparency!)

Stock Photographs

As I stated earlier, Stock photographs are taken by other people of other things than those that directly relate to your business, but that doesn't mean you can't use them... a LOT! The key, though, is to use them for the right reasons.

If you are writing a general article about your products or the kinds of customers you serve, then a stock photo may be appropriate. If you are a personal trainer, then showing stock images of people doing chin ups, running, or lifting weights might get your message across just fine. If you're trying to make a point about diets, then a picture of a chocolate cake might be ideal. It's okay to be creative, but try not to be too obscure. The image you choose should make people feel something about your subject matter in that particular article.

The beautiful thing about the sites I mentioned above is that they all now offer stock photos, stock graphics... and stock VIDEO! This is huge. I was just able to do a background video for a coffee shop using entirely free stock video from one of the websites I mentioned. Stupid easy, and free for the customer.

Video

As I just mentioned, you don't even have to shoot
your own video to make video for your content. You
have to use the same parameters, however, for using
stock video that you use for stock photos. Make sure it's
relevant! Capturing attention is great... but you really do
need to make sure it relates in some way to your product
or service, or it just feels like a cheap bait and switch.
Best example: Cute Cat Videos. If you're not running a
vet clinic, or an adoption service, or a pet sitting
service... the cat videos aren't what you need to be
running. Sure, they'll go viral, but just like the free
coffee cups, the quality of the traffic will be less than
zero. Seriously.

Let's take the coffee shop example I used. Certainly
when I made the background video for the homepage it
was great for the "flavor" of the site. High class. Totally
about coffee beans and espresso machines and steaming
cups of coffee on non-identifiable tabletops. That all
served the purpose of establishing the branding image of
the shop. But I could've taken the same videos, added
some text or narration over them about new hours, or
how early we are there for people who need to get to
work... and bam! We have social media content. Make it
short, and it becomes a Facebook Reel.

I'm going to toss out a couple creative ideas here to
let maybe get your imagination working. If you install

air conditioners, and it's July in Florida, how about a picture of a beautiful winter snowscape? Maybe penguins playing on an iceberg? "Some people don't need air conditioning. You're in Florida. We've got you covered."

Another idea: You own a shoe store. Find stock video of people walking down the street. Just their feet. I just went to Pixabay and put in "street feet" and got three videos. Two won't work. One will, for sure. Just match it up with a good set of graphics, some stock music, and Voila! You have video footage for an ad or Reel.

Naturally, you can shoot your own video of your own product or showroom, but don't let the inability to get that video done by a professional become your excuse for hamstringing your business marketing program. If you have a new product in, shoot some photos. But then set the same product up and shoot a video of it by moving the camera around it to give a 360 degree view of the item. I remember one product had had an amazing sparkle-coated image that just didn't show up in photos. But the video was incredible! Motion grabs attention SO much better and faster than a still image, and your phone gives you the ability to become a complete video production house in seconds.

Make sure your quality is decent. If you're shooting video, make sure the background sound isn't distracting or worse… offensive. A drill press in the background can be horrific if somebody is wearing earphones, or somebody using vulgar language that gets blasted on a work computer can be devastating to YOUR business… and someone's career! Don't be that business. Pay attention to your audio. If you have great video, but there's problems with the audio, use an editor to drop the audio and add royalty free music. You guessed it: Pixabay has free music as well.

Now that we've mentioned that, let's dive into the next topic: Audio.

Audio

The audio version of multi-media has taken off ridiculously in the last ten years. We call them "podcasts", and you can do amazing things with your customer base if you really have the chutzpah to engage in a consistent manner on a variety of related topics.

When I hear the word "podcast", I think about the 60 or 90 minute productions by big names like Joe Rogan or Simon Sinek. Massive production value. A whole crew of people managing the sound quality, cuts, commercial breaks, music… oh my GOD! You don't have those kinds of resources or time available! You can't make a podcast!

Well, let's step back a bit. Where is it written that a podcast has to be 90 minutes long? Nowhere. There is no time limit. It doesn't even have to be an even number of minutes. It just has to be enough to cover the topic you are promising in a length that your prospective customer is willing to invest in hearing about it.

One of my favorite podcasts, for example, is literally called "5 Minute Marketing". It's nothing spectacular, but I love the fact that I know I'm not committing more than 5 minutes of my time to possibly learn something new about e-commerce. Now they've only been running two episodes a month since July of 2019, but they've done exactly the right thing with it: They've kept their promise. It's 5 minutes. It's every two weeks. And it's on topic.

Seriously. Five minutes every two weeks. And the sound quality, although excellent, isn't that hard to recreate with a $90 microphone from BestBuy and a quiet office with just you and your laptop. Heck, you can use your phone if you have to, but make sure you experiment a lot with it to get the angle and distance optimized for great sound quality.

And then you open up a podcasting account on Spotify (used to be Anchor) and away you go. You can be active on Spotify in just a few minutes. And then what do you do? You don't actually go live right away. You can schedule your releases ahead of time. Do it. Get 3 or 4 podcasts ahead, and THEN start releasing them one at a time. That way you are under NO pressure to produce a podcast "this week!", and you can always be working a month or two ahead.

All the pressure is gone now. You have your podcast on Posture and Exercise, or Solar Power for your Home, or Simple Car Maintenance Tips, or Kitchen Gadget Reviews. It doesn't matter. The topic is yours to create.

I looked at creating a podcast recently, and decided to see if I would have enough content to make it worth doing. I know one professional (and VERY successful!) YouTuber who did the same exercise, thinking he would only need 5 or 6 topics to "test" his new podcast idea. He was wrong. You may only have 5 or 6 total ideas. When I did my research, I looked at having a YEAR of weekly content available. 50 ideas. 50 subjects. It started general, and then those generalizations became categories. Once I had my categories, it was easy to keep putting in details that would need to be fleshed out in a 5-10 minute episode every week. In an hour I had 50 topics. Yes, I could do the podcast.

Then, when I looked at the topics, I asked myself if I was really interested in devoting the time to deliver these to my clients over the next year. Were these things they would really want to know. Well, the answer was actually, "no". I've made very successful podcasts, and I could tell that this wasn't going to be one of them. So I killed the idea, and moved on to another one. No testing. Nothing wasted but a few hours, and those saved me weeks of effort on a project I ultimately knew I wasn't going to enjoy working on.

Yes, it's okay to say no.

But don't stop there. If you have customers who ask a lot of questions, then you have the perfect opportunity for a podcast. Deal with one question a week.

If you need to be more visual, then take your podcast to Rumble or YouTube. Make sure you have REALLY good audio equipment, and your smartphone will probably be all the video equipment you need.

I have some wireless lavalieres that bluetooth to my iPhone. The sound quality is amazing, and I can be up to 50 feet away from my phone and still have crystal clear audio. The internal software silences wind noise as well. And they cost about $20 on eBay. Clip it to your collar and you're ready to be a YouTube star.

There are entire courses available online for becoming a YouTuber. I suggest finding a few and testing them out. Literally you can go to YouTube and search "How to make a YouTube video", and one of the first things that pops up is a course for beginners from EpidemicSound. They provide background music, so they want you to sign up for their service. The best way for them to get customers is to create them! So their course is probably pretty solid and will get you a long way toward understanding intros and outros. It's almost 2 hours long, but broken up into segments that you can consume in brain-sized pieces.

Any way you look at it, multimedia marketing is incredibly powerful, exciting, and honestly, can be quite fun. It's not as hard as you think, and there are a ton of resources out there to help you get started, and keep getting better.

Your business bank account will thank you.

The Sixth Driver

Wait. What? I thought there were only five drivers? What gives? Did I lie to you? Have I broken my headline promise?

No, not really, because if you've been paying attention through this whole book, you'll have seen the Sixth Driver is right there in every chapter.

The Sixth Driver is *you*.

It is up to you to take personal responsibility for the marketing of your business. It is up to you to set the tone of communication with your prospective clients. It is up to you to utilize your experience and knowledge of your products and your customers to give them the information you know they need before they make a buying decision. It is up to you to be the face of your business. People don't buy from your business... they buy from you. A business is just a legal construct to help the IRS and attorneys understand who is responsible for the bank accounts, and little more. But **your** business is a personal relationship between you and your customers.

Online marketing allows you to reach out and have that relationship with a vastly greater number of people than you could meet with every week on your own. You can only do so many networking meetings before you have to get back to running the business side of your business.

But a well crafted digital marketing program, run through a well engineered Online Marketing Platform, will give you the ability to run this entire program in as little as 30 minutes a day. Really, that's all it takes. If you do any more than that, it's because you are finding it wildly successful, or you're just having a blast making your videos, having guests on your podcast, or using Canva to make really cool memes that feature your creations. But that's up to you.

It's all up to you. Your business needs you. You are your dream's best evangelist. And if you take on this challenge of running a business in today's world, you had better be ready to handle this kind of marketing, because it has been the biggest indicator of success or failure I've seen. Start it, stick with it, and keep improving. It is not a finished product, but a constant set of scientific experiments meant to keep getting better and better results from your efforts.

But nothing happens until you start.

We all know that a journey of a thousand miles begins with a single step. I'm here to congratulate you on taking the first step already, by reading this book to learn where you must step next.

Bon voyage.